CREATIVE
BEAD
WEAVING

This page
NANC MEINHARDT
Shades of a Different Color
see page 112

Facing page
KATHY SEELY
Connections
see page 64

CREATIVE BEAD WEAVING

A CONTEMPORARY GUIDE TO CLASSIC OFF-LOOM STITCHES

CAROL WILCOX WELLS

LARK BOOKS

A Division of Sterling Publishing Co., Inc.
New York

EDITOR: **Carol Taylor**
ART DIRECTOR: **Chris Bryant**
PHOTOGRAPHER: **Evan Bracken**
ILLUSTRATOR: **Carol Wilcox Wells**

Library of Congress Cataloging-in-Publication Data
Wells, Carol Wilcox.
    Creative bead weaving : a contemporary guide
to classic off-loom stitches / Carol Wilcox Wells.
        p.   cm.
    Includes bibliographical references and index.
    ISBN 1-57990-080-1
    1. Beadwork.   I. Title
TT860.W45   1996
745.58'2—dc20   96-18875
                            CIP

20 19 18 17 16 15 14 13

Published by Lark Books, A Division of
Sterling Publishing Co., Inc.
387 Park Avenue South, New York, N.Y. 10016

First Paperback Edition 1998
© 1996 by Carol Wilcox Wells

Distributed in Canada by Sterling Publishing,
c/o Canadian Manda Group, 165 Dufferin Street
Toronto, Ontario, Canada M6K 3H6

Distributed in the United Kingdom by GMC Distribution Services,
Castle Place, 166 High Street, Lewes, East Sussex, England BN7 1XU

Distributed in Australia by Capricorn Link (Australia) Pty Ltd.,
P.O. Box 704, Windsor, NSW 2756 Australia

If you have questions or comments about this book, please contact:
Lark Books, 67 Broadway, Asheville, NC 28801, (828) 253-0467

Manufactured in China

ISBN 13: 978-1-57990-080-9
ISBN 10: 1-57990-080-1

For information about custom editions, special sales, premium and corporate purchases, please contact Sterling Special Sales Department at 800-805-5489 or specialsales@sterlingpub.com.

right
ANN PAXTON
Queen of Heaven,
amulet purse, 7 in. x 2¼ in. x ¼ in. (18 cm x 5.5 cm x .5 cm), peyote stitch; the five-bead-wide strap reads "Queen of Heaven, comfort of men and bliss of angels, Divine Mother and Blessed Virgin Mary." The beads are 11° cylinder seed beads.

Contents

Introduction 6

1 Tips, Tools, and Materials 8

2 Peyote Stitch 12

3 Brick Stitch 64

4 Square Stitch 82

5 Right-Angle Weave 94

6 African Helix, Netting, and Chevron Chain 104

7 Combining Stitches 118

Contributing Artists 142

Acknowledgments 144

Bibliography 144

Index 144

A Note About Suppliers 144

"I'll give my jewels for a set of beads..."

~William Shakespeare
Richard II

Introduction

For millennia, people from diverse cultures have prized the rich colors and intriguing patterns of small beads woven together into a more or less solid "fabric." By 2200 B.C., the Egyptians were using what is now called peyote stitch to weave beaded belts, bands, ceremonial aprons, and burial garments. The people of Malaysia used bead netting to fashion jackets, headbands, and baby carriers. Europeans have adorned themselves and their homes with beads for generations. It's no accident that historical beadwork is displayed in museums around the world.

On an individual level, I suspect that most of us have a beader or two somewhere in the branches of our family tree. My great great great grandmother and my great great grandmother were both bead weavers, and I have inherited a collection of antique beads, several beaded purses, and their love of this endlessly fascinating craft.

This book is an invitation to join the long, gorgeous tradition of beadwork. My focus is on the classic techniques for weaving beads without a loom—techniques that have been handed down for generations. Peyote stitch, brick stitch, square stitch, and right-angle weave are covered nuance by nuance. African helix, netting, and chevron chain are also included but in somewhat less detail.

The last chapter explains how to move easily from one stitch to another, in order to combine several stitches in the same piece. Using multiple stitches is increasingly popular today, but it is far from new. Note the English basket (*below*), which dates from 1670.

Each stitch is presented in three ways. First, there are complete instructions that explain how to work the stitch in all

ENGLISH BEADED BASKET,
circa 1670; 19½ in. x 26¼ in. (49.5 cm x 66.5 cm); heavy wire frame covered with blue and white beads strung on wire in a spiral pattern. The sides of the basket are decorated with beaded leaves in right-angle weave. The bottom consists of bead embroidery and off-loom beadwork on white satin The stems and the clothing are peyote stitch. Note that much of the beadwork is three-dimensional.
COLLECTION OF THE COLONIAL WILLIAMSBURG FOUNDATION, WILLIAMSBURG, VIRGINIA.

DETAIL, ENGLISH BEADED BASKET.
Colonial Williamsburg Foundation.

its important variations—flat or tubular, for example. While the text is, I hope, useful and as clear as I could make it, I have long believed that showing is the best form of teaching. So, drawing upon my background as a graphic artist and on my newfound computer skills, I have illustrated the text with about 200 drawings.

The second means of learning a stitch is to make something with it. So for each stitch there is at least one project, complete with detailed instructions; for most stitches, there are several. As the most popular stitch among contemporary beaders, peyote has the most projects.

Photos of handsome beadwork by talented contemporary beaders accompany each stitch. While there are no how-to instructions for these pieces, there is much to be learned—about color, form, ideas, and creativity.

While the end results are basically the same, beaders vary in how they work—how they hold the needle and thread, for example, and whether they work peyote stitch from top to bottom or from bottom to top. The book explains how I bead and how I teach others to bead, but there are many ways to work and I would not presume to say that one way is better than the other.

There is less leeway when it comes to craftsmanship. It is so very important that every bead be right. Every element is part of the whole, and if the finished work is to be spectacular, so should every individual bead. The same is true of finishing a piece. If you have spent hours weaving a brooch or evening purse, then it deserves a carefully attached finding or a well-sewn lining. Go to extremes for perfection and take pride in your work; the effort will come back to you.

Our heritage of bead weaving is a formidable one, one that we draw on whether we are conscious of it or not. The instinct to weave together, be it our lives or our beads, is too strong to break, and I for one am glad.

~Carol Wilcox Wells

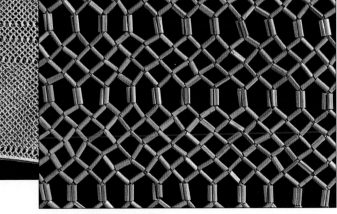

CHINESE VEST OF BAMBOO BEADS, *late 19th century, bead netting; 19 in. x 21½ in. (48.5 cm x 54.5 cm). The individual beads measure ¼ in. x ¹⁄₁₆ in. (.5 cm x .16 cm). This vest was probably worn over a light cotton undergarment and under an outer garment. It provided the wearer with ventilation and protected the clothing from perspiration.*
COLLECTION OF VALERIE HECTOR.
PHOTO: CHRIS CASSIDY.

DETAIL, CHINESE BAMBOO VEST.

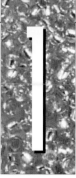

1 Materials, Tools, and Tips

Regardless of the stitch or the project, you will need beads, needles, and thread. Depending on what you're making, you may require a few other tools as well.

Beads

The beads used throughout this book are glass seed beads of various shapes and sizes. The only exception is the clay vessel on page 80, which uses African clay beads.

Seed beads are sized by number; the higher the number, the smaller the bead. Contemporary bead manufactures produce size 6° through size 15° in a wide range of colors and finishes. A simple transparent bead can be frosted (matte), color-lined, silver-lined, or copper-lined. Its finish can be luster, gold luster, or iridescent (often called iris, rainbow, or aurora borealis). Opaque beads can also have matte, luster, iridescent, galvanized, metallic, and gilded finishes.

The shapes of seed beads are equally varied. To name just a few, there are round beads with round holes, round beads with square holes, triangular beads, cylinders, hexagons (also known as two-cut beads), and charlottes (which have one facet cut into the surface).

The Japanese cylinder seed bead has become a favorite of many beaders for peyote stitch and many other off-loom techniques. This bead is very consistent in size and has very large holes, both of which make working with it a pleasure.

Bugle beads—long, cylindrical beads—come in many of the same finishes as seed beads. They range from 2 mm to 30 mm in length and vary in width. (Traditionally, beads are measured in millimeters. Don't be unnerved if you're accustomed to inches; after examining a few beads, you'll adjust quickly.) While most bugles are smooth and straight, some are twisted.

The Size of a Seed Bead

Seed bead sizes are often written with what looks like a degree symbol—for example, size 6°, size 11°. Why this odd notation? The answer comes to us from Waltraud Neuwirth in *Beads from Gablonz* (Vienna, 1994).

Years ago, when mass production of beads was in its infancy, manufacturers chose the most common bead they produced as the "null bead" and labeled it size 0. Larger beads were given increasingly larger numbers: 2, 3, 4, etc. When manufacturers began to make smaller beads that resembled seeds, they labeled the next size smaller than the null bead as size 00; the next smaller, 000; the next smaller, 0000. Obviously, such a system became cumbersome fairly quickly, so a shorthand was developed to specify the number of 0s: 6/0, 11/0, etc—which evolved into the current 6° and 11°.

TOP TO BOTTOM: *3.3 matte purple cylinders, 15° gold hex-cuts, three colors of 11° cylinder seed beads (purple, silver, and red), 15° chartreuse round seed beads, 6° purple seed beads, 3 mm cream bugle beads, 9 mm matte blue-purple bugles, 13° gold charlottes*

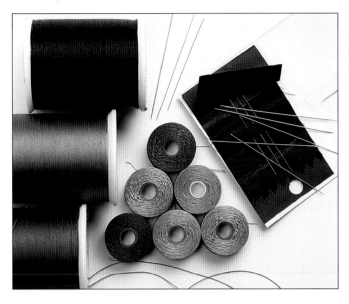

Beading needles in various sizes, along with two kinds of beading thread. The thread on the bobbins has multiple linear (untwisted) strands. On the spools is twisted multifilament thread.

Thread

There are many threads on the market that can be used for beading. Two of the best were originally manufactured for the upholstery industry and are now widely used in the beading world. One of them, a linear (untwisted) multifilament, comes on a bobbin and is offered in many colors and sizes. Size D is especially strong and versatile. The other thread of choice comes on a spool; it's a heavy-duty twisted multifilament, which makes needle threading a little more difficult. Both threads are available almost anywhere beads and beading supplies are sold.

As for color, try to match the thread to the beads. Keep in mind that the color of the thread will affect the color of any transparent bead in the piece you are working on. As an unlikely example, a transparent blue bead woven on gold thread would acquire a greenish cast.

Needles

Beading needles come in several sizes: 10, 12, 13, 15, and 16. The larger the number, the smaller the needle. These needles are approximately 2 inches (5 cm) long, and sizes 13 through 16 are fairly flexible. A size 12 needle seems to be the most versatile; it can be used with size 11° round and cylinder seed beads and any bead that is larger. Use the 13s, 15s, and 16s for smaller beads.

Many beaders use the shorter quilting needles called "betweens," but I find them a bit awkward. Use the needle that you are most comfortable with—one that is relatively easy to thread and that will pass through a bead several times.

Bead Dish

Beaders use a remarkable variety of surfaces and dishes to hold their beads for a given project, and I'm no exception. Personally, I have found that a low-sided china dish is the best. My favorite variety is a rectangular china watercolor tray with five round wells and five slanted ones. My second choice would be the white china coasters available at import stores. Plastic lids from some food products fit snugly over these coasters, making them ideal for traveling.

Plastic watercolor trays tend to build up static, and the beads begin to have a life of their own; the plastic trays are also very lightweight and the beads spill easily. Putting the beads on a piece of suede works quite well—unless you have cats that rule the roost and walk across your work area whenever they please.

Assorted Tools

The following tools are occasionally essential and frequently helpful.

CHAIN-NOSE PLIERS (round on the outside and flat on the inside) can help pull a needle through a tight spot and are often used to add jewelry "findings" (clasps and fasteners) to a finished piece of beadwork. They're also useful for breaking a bead—frequently the quickest and easiest way to remove a bead that's been woven in the wrong place.

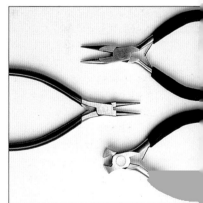

CLOCKWISE FROM LEFT:
round-nose pliers,
chain-nose pliers,
flush cutters for cutting wire.

ROUND-NOSE PLIERS (curved on both inside and outside surfaces) can be used to form loops on the ends of wire findings.

FLUSH CUTTERS are useful for cutting wire; a file can be used to smooth the rough ends.

PAPER AND PENCIL are invaluable in designing a piece, either on plain paper or on a bead graph, and in keeping a record of the project as you work on it. I like to write down the time spent and all of the supplies used--beads (color, sizes, and quantities), findings, and thread--and make notes on the process and any new ideas.

A METAL BOARD WITH MAGNETIC STRIPS holds a beading graph in place and helps keep track of where you are if the design is a complicated one.

CALCULATOR. There is a definite mathematical aspect to bead weaving, and I, for one, can use all the help I can get.

GLUE. A flexible, styrene-based adhesive effectively bonds leather, glass, and metal. It comes in large tubes and is available wherever beading supplies are sold.

Top to bottom: a barrette back, a head pin, a length of chain attached to a head pin. Next row, left to right: clasps, jump rings (wire rings for linking bead-work to findings), French ear wires, ear posts, and a pin back. Bottom: a length of pur-chased chain.

Findings

Findings are metal components used as attachments and fasteners for jewelry. They are mass-produced and readily available at bead stores and craft shops. There are many levels of quality. The least expensive are made of yellow or white metal-plated brass or nickel; more expensive are sterling silver and karat gold. Use the best that your pocketbook will allow.

Ending a Thread

Unless your project is very tiny, you will use many pieces of thread before you are through. When you near the end of a given thread, end it before it is too short to work with. If possible, end it in the middle of a row so that you know exactly where you are if you are following a graph.

Figure 1. Following the diagonal line of beads, weave the thread through several beads, moving up and to the left from the last bead added. Catch the threads between beads and make a small loop. Pass the needle through the loop twice and pull slowly to form a small knot that sits on the threads between the beads. Moving on the same diagonal, weave through four more beads, pulling the knot into a bead. Knot again and weave through more beads. Pull on the thread and cut it as close to the work as possible.

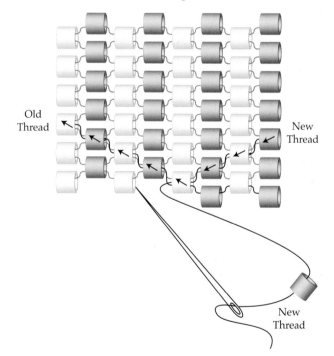

Adding a Thread

To add a new thread (see Figure 1 again), weave it in from the right side of the work, then knot, weave, knot, and weave out of the bead needed to begin again. Try to space the knots in different areas of the work.

Making Fringe

I've never seen a fringe I didn't like! (I have seen a few that I wish I'd thought of myself.) With its free-swinging strands of beads, fringe adds movement to woven beadwork. It's also an ideal place to add those one-of-a-kind beads to your one-of-a-kind piece.

Fringe enjoys great variety. Straight fringe, the simplest type, is child's play. String on the desired number of beads. Then, skipping the last bead, take the needle back up the row. Other fringes are just variations on this simple theme. (Attaching fringe to woven beadwork is discussed in later chapters on specific stitches.)

In choosing a fringe, you'll need to make a number of decisions. How long do you want the fringe to be? How many rows? Will all rows be the same length? Will the fringe have a pattern, made by color placement? Will the fringe hang from the bottom, the top, or the sides? What beads will be used? What style fringe will be used?

Figure 2. Several styles of fringe are very popular. Top row, left to right: straight, straight with a loop, figure 8, circular. Bottom row, left to right: circular with straights and loops, branched, straight with loops. These are just a few of the options. Be creative, and remember that fringe is fun.

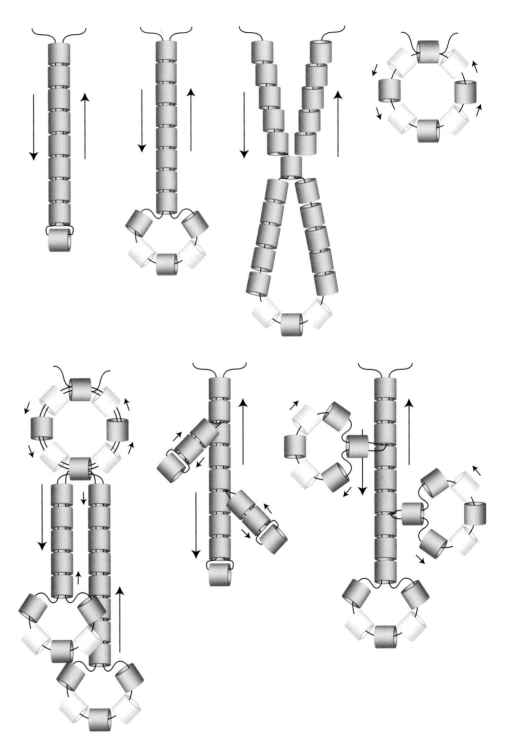

2

Peyote Stitch

An ancient and honored stitch, peyote is probably the most popular off-loom stitch among contemporary beaders. It is simple to weave, yet amazingly versatile.

Peyote has many nuances—most of them, I hope, covered here. In addition to the tips and techniques, there are nine projects to try—some very simple and a few, shall we say, intense. Enjoy them all.

 JODY STEWART-KELLER
Goddesses,
earrings, 2¼ in. x 1 in. (5.5 cm x 2.5 cm), peyote stitch, 15° seed beads;
Rectangular Barrette, 3½ in. x 1 in. (9 cm x 2.5 cm), peyote stitch, 15° seed beads.

do by picture not words

Flat Peyote

If you're a beginning beader, try starting with size 11° cylinder seed beads. Their shape makes the beads easier to position and the pattern easier to see.

EVEN-COUNT FLAT PEYOTE

Figure 1. String a bead on the thread and loop through it again, leaving a 6-inch (15 cm) tail. Add beads until you reach the width you want, making sure that your total is an even number.

Figure 2. To start the next row, pick up another bead and take the needle through the second bead from the end. In the example shown, pick up bead #9 and go through bead #7.

Figure 3. Pick up bead #10 and stitch through bead #5. Keep the tension tight enough to produce peyote's vertical brick pattern but not so tight as to make the work stiff. Continue across until you reach the end of this row.

Figure 4. To turn and go back across in the opposite direction, pick up bead #13 and stitch through the last bead in the previous row, #12. Continue in this manner until the desired length is reached.

COUNTING ROWS

In peyote stitch, rows are counted on the diagonal. In the example above, the first eight beads that were strung on the thread became rows 1 and 2 when subsequent weaving pushed and pulled them into their bricklike pattern. At Figure 3, you worked the third row of peyote, counting on the diagonal: count beads #8, #7, and #10, for example, or beads #6, #5, and #11. For more explanation of counting on the diagonal, see Using a Peyote Graph, page 32.

NOTE: For the sake of clarity, all of the illustrations are shown with spaces between the beads. In the actual weaving, there are no such spaces.

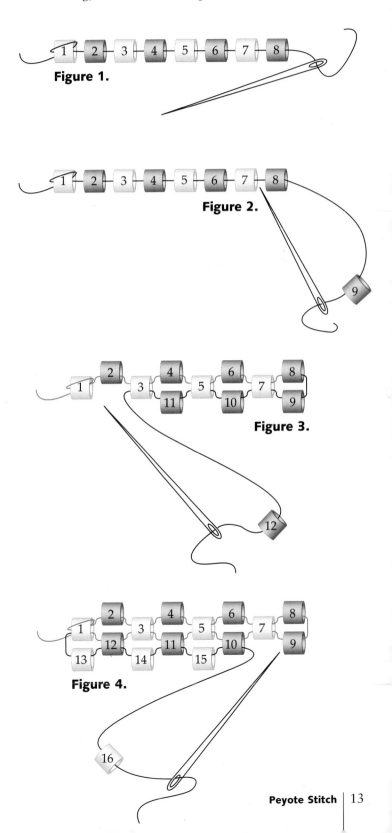

Figure 1.

Figure 2.

Figure 3.

Figure 4.

ODD-COUNT FLAT PEYOTE

For a pattern with a center point, you must use an odd number of beads. On one side, odd-count uses the simple turn used in even-count peyote and shown in Figure 2. The other side requires a slightly more intricate turn.

Figure 5. String one bead on the thread and loop through it again, leaving a 6-inch (15 cm) tail. Add beads until you reach the width you want, making sure that your total is an odd number. You will work the tail into the piece later.

Figure 6. To start the next row—row 3, counting on the diagonal—pick up bead #10 and stitch through bead #8. We'll call this Turn A. Pick up bead #11 and stitch through bead #6; pick up bead #12 and stitch through bead #4. Now pick up bead #13 and pass the needle through beads #2 and #1. Keep the tension tight enough to produce the vertical brick pattern but not so tight as to make the work stiff.

Figure 7. Pick up bead #14 (the last bead of the third row) and weave through beads #2, #3, #13, back through #2, #1, and #14. The dark line on the drawing shows the way; you are doing a figure eight. This is how Turn B is done at the beginning of a piece. You are now ready to begin the next row with bead #15.

Figure 8. Continue to weave. When you pick up bead #22, pass the needle through beads #15 and #14. Now pick up #23 and pass the needle through #15, #2, #14, and #23. You are now ready to begin the next row with bead #24.

In odd-count flat peyote, there will always be an easy turn (Turn A) on one side and a hard weaving turn (Turn B) on the other. When doing the hard turn at the beginning of a piece, you weave through three vertical rows (rows A, B, and C in Figure 8). Every hard turn thereafter, the weaving is done through two vertical rows (A and B).

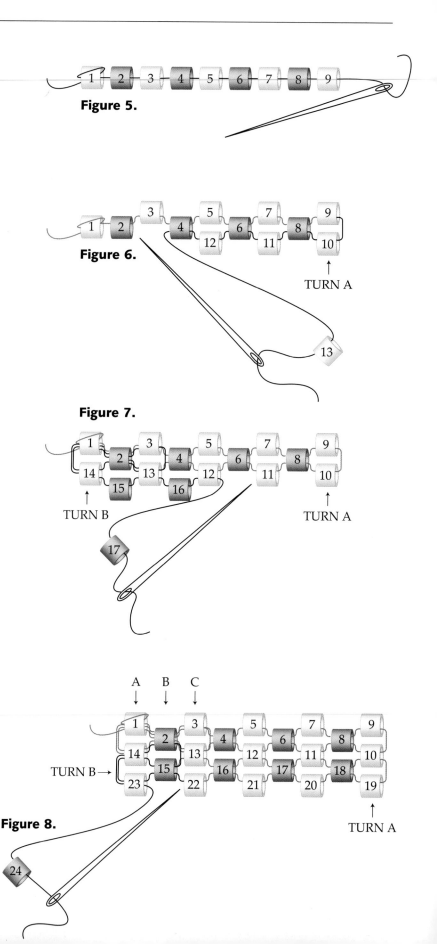

Figure 5.

Figure 6.

TURN A

Figure 7.

TURN B   TURN A

A   B   C

TURN B →

Figure 8.

TURN A

A NOTE ABOUT TENSION

When you begin a peyote piece, the first bead is looped onto the thread partly to keep the remaining beads from falling off but also to help maintain the tension when adding the next row.

At times, the beads become loose and need to be tightened up. To do that, just slide the initial looped bead up the thread to tighten the row.

When the piece is completed, undo that first loop of thread so there's no unsightly thread on the outside of the bead. Attach a needle to the initial tail thread tail and weave it into the piece.

CYNTHIA CUNNINGHAM
Mendocino Summer, *necklace, 6 in. x 2 in. (15 cm x 5 cm), peyote stitch, 11° seed beads, coral, pearls, and beach glass.*

Tubular Peyote

Tubular peyote is worked three-dimensionally. It can be worked on a removable form, such as a cardboard tube from a roll of paper towels, or around objects such as wooden beads and glass vessels. It can also be done with no supporting form at all.

EVEN-COUNT TUBULAR PEYOTE

Thread a needle and string on an even number of beads. The count will depend on the circumference of the object that you are beading around. Do not loop or knot the first bead.

Figures 9 and 10. Slide the beads to within 6 inches (15 cm) of the end of the thread. Tie the thread ends together, using two square knots and leaving a two- to three-bead space of thread bare. Slip the ring of beads over a tube to support the work. (The initial ring of beads will become rows 1 and 2 when the third row of beads is added, pulling the ring of beads into their up-and-down positions.)

Figure 11. Spread the beads so they are evenly spaced around the form. To start the next row, take the needle through the first bead to the left of the knot. Pick up a bead, skip a bead on the ring, and go through the next bead. Pull the thread down tight enough so that the bead you are adding pushes the bead above it halfway up the neighboring beads. Continue around until you are back where you started.

Figure 12. When ending row 3, pass the needle through the first bead of row 2 and the first bead of row 3. You are now ready to begin row 4. Each time you end a row, your needle will pass through the first bead of the preceding row and the first bead of the row you are on.

NOTE: The first bead of every row will move one bead to the left. When following a graph, use this diagonal line as a reference point.

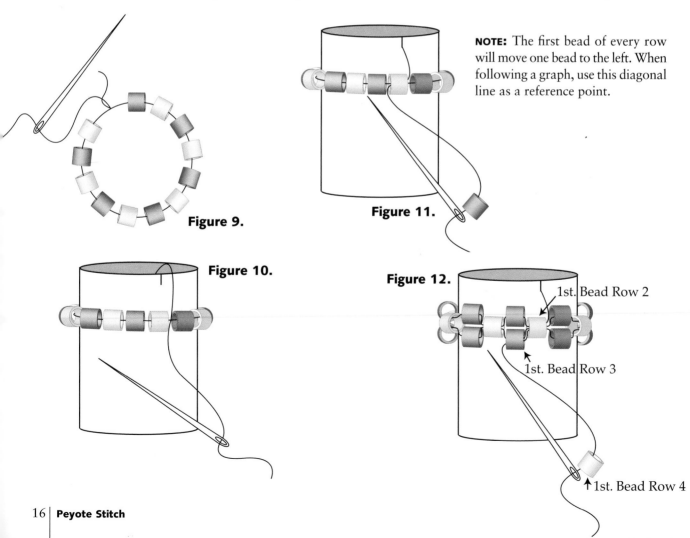

Figure 9.

Figure 10.

Figure 11.

Figure 12.

1st. Bead Row 2

1st. Bead Row 3

↑1st. Bead Row 4

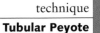

ODD-COUNT
TUBULAR PEYOTE

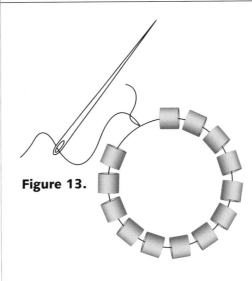

Figure 13.

Figure 13. String on an odd number of beads. The count will depend on the circumference of the object you are beading around. Leaving a 6-inch (15 cm) tail, tie the thread ends together, using two square knots. Leave a two- to three-bead space of bare thread if you want a softer feel to the work.

Figure 14. Slip the ring of beads over a tube to support the work. Spread the beads so that they are evenly spaced around the form. This space will be taken up as beads are added to the next row.

Figure 14.

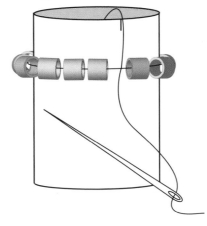

Figure 15. To start row 3, go through the first bead to the left of the knot, pick up a bead, skip a bead on the ring, and go through the next bead. Pull the thread down tight enough so that the bead you are adding pushes the bead above it halfway up the neighboring beads. Continue around until you are back where you started.

To begin the next row (row 4), pass the needle through the first bead of row 3.

Odd-count tubular peyote spirals down the tube; there will never be a straight edge across the work. One bead will always be taller than the rest.

Note that the first bead of each successive row moves over one bead to the left, as in even-count tubular peyote.

Figure 15.

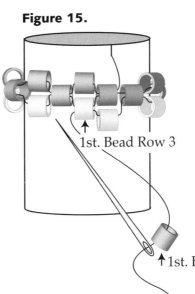

1st. Bead Row 3

↑1st. Bead Row 4

CAROL WILCOX WELLS

Spring, *amulet purse, 4 in. x 2¼ in. x ¼ in. (10 cm x 5.5 cm x .5 cm), peyote stitch, 11° cylinder seed beads and other assorted beads.*

DUMMY ROWS

I always start tubular peyote with three "dummy" rows—
rows that don't count because I will remove them after a
inch (2.5 cm) of weaving. Why? The first beads are on on
ring of thread; they always tend to pull in and be somewha
tighter than the rest of the work. Moreover, on a very com
plicated pattern, it's easier to count and string the first rov
if you don't have to worry about the color of the beads.

DENEEN MATSON
Forever Beading I,
12 in. x 11½ in. (30.5 cm x 29 cm),
peyote stitch, 11° cylinder seed beads.

CAROL WILCOX WELLS
Flower of Aphrodite,
evening purse, 12 in. x 5 in. (30.5 cm x 12.5 cm)
diameter, peyote stitch, Ultrasuede lining,
satin cord, 11° cylinder seed beads.

MORE NOTES ABOUT TENSION

Tension is very important in tubular peyote, and it must be right from the beginning. If you are making a basket that will have to stand on its own, the tension will need to be very tight from the start; don't leave any spaces in the initial ring of beads. On the other hand, if you are making something supple, such as an evening purse, then you will need to leave a two- to three-bead space of bare thread in that initial ring. This space will be used up by the next row of beads as they force the first beads up into position, making the vertical brick pattern that is peyote stitch.

LINDA FIFIELD
Fire Flies,
*vessel, 4 in. x 3 in. x 3 in.
(10 cm x 7.5 cm x 7.5 cm),
peyote stitch on lathe-turned
wooden vessel, branched fringe,
10° seed beads.*

Increasing

Increasing peyote stitch—adding extra beads to make the piece wider—can be done in a variety of ways.

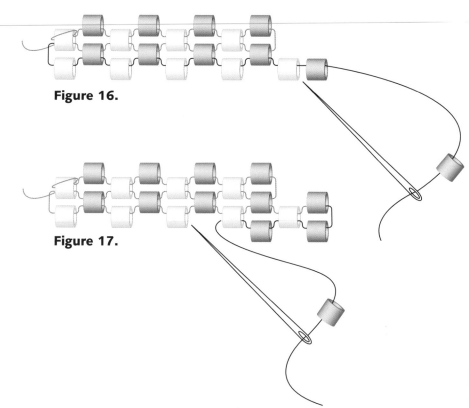

Figure 16.

INCREASING ON OUTSIDE EDGES BY AN EVEN NUMBER OF BEADS

Figure 16. Pick up the quantity of beads desired at the end of the row (an even number). Here we are increasing by two beads. Then pick up another bead (the first bead of the next row), turn, skip a bead and go into the next bead.

Figure 17. Continue with regular peyote stitch. The width of the piece has increased from eight to 10 beads across.

Figure 17.

INCREASING ON OUTSIDE EDGES BY AN ODD NUMBER OF BEADS

Increasing an odd number of vertical rows is somewhat harder, because you have to weave back into the piece to stabilize the new row and then get back into position to begin again.

Figure 18. To increase by one vertical row, pick up two beads (#25 and #26) and go back into bead #17.

Figure 19. Continue weaving through beads #9, #25, and #26. You are now ready to begin the next row with bead #27.

Figure 20. To increase by an odd number larger than one, pick up the three increase beads (#25, #26, #27) and bead #28. Pass the needle into bead #26.

Figure 21. Pick up bead #29 and weave through #17, #9, #25, #26, #27, and #28. You are now ready to begin the next row with bead #30.

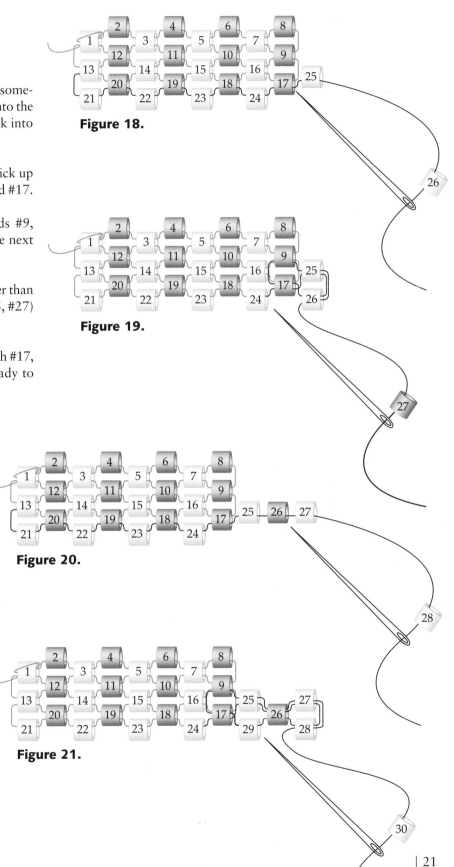

Figure 18.

Figure 19.

Figure 20.

Figure 21.

CAROL WILCOX WELLS
Under the Rose,
*evening purse, 6 in. x 4 in. x 1½ in.
(15 cm x 10 cm x 4 cm),
peyote stitch, 11° cylinder
seed beads, silk cord and tassels.*

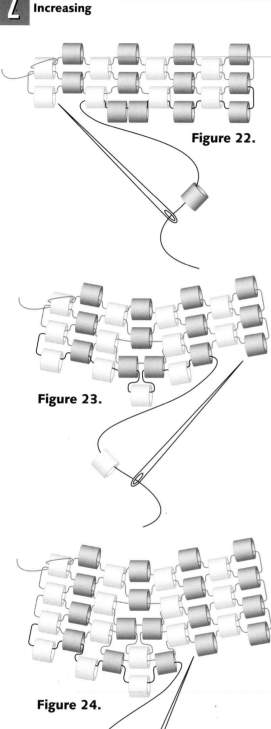

Figure 22.

Figure 23.

Figure 24.

CYNTHIA RUTLEDGE
Garden Urn,
*amulet purse, 3 in. x 2¼ in.
diameter (7.5 cm x 5.5 cm),
peyote stitch, 11° cylinder
seed beads and other
assorted beads.*

INCREASING WITHIN A PIECE

When increasing within flat peyote, the work will flare out at the sides. Increasing within tubular peyote will cause the piece to flare out toward you.

Figure 22. Pick up two beads instead of one in a single space.

Figure 23. On the next row, add a bead between the two beads that were put on at the point of increase.

Figure 24. Note the effect after another row and a half have been added. The vertical rows have increased by two, making the piece 10 beads wide instead of eight.

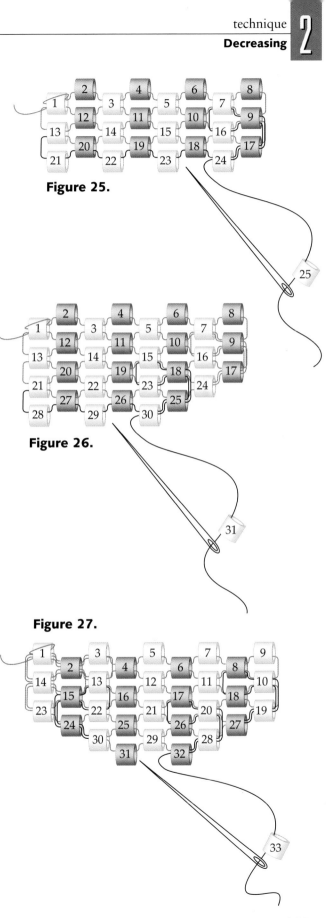

Figure 25.

Figure 26.

Figure 27.

Decreasing

Decreasing a peyote piece—adding fewer beads in order to make it narrower—can be done in a variety of ways.

DECREASING ON THE OUTSIDE EDGES

This is done by omitting beads at the end of a row—which leaves you no place to go. You must weave back into the body of the piece to get back into position to continue.

Figure 25. After bead #24 is added, the needle will be coming out of bead #17, pointing to the right. Pass the needle into beads #9, #16, #7, #9, #17, and #24. You are now ready to begin the next row with bead #25.

Figure 26. Continue across and back, ending with bead #30. The needle will be coming out of bead #25, pointing to the right. To decrease again, forming a diagonal line, pass the needle through beads #18, #23, #15, #18, #25, and #30. You are now ready to begin the next row with bead #31.

Figure 27. This illustration shows an odd number of beads being decreased into a point. It is done in the same manner as shown in Figures 25 and 26, except that the decreasing occurs on both sides. Since some of the beads will have many threads going through them, you may find it easier to switch to a smaller needle.

DECREASING WITHIN A PIECE

Figure 28. To decrease, simply skip a space where a bead should go. Pull the thread tight to close the gap between the beads.

Figure 29. On the next row, add one bead in the decreased space.

Figure 30. Continue with peyote stitch. Two vertical rows have been decreased by the dropping of one bead. The illustration started with eight beads across; it now has six.

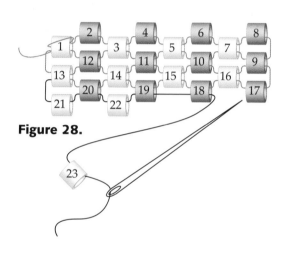

Figure 28.

Figure 29.

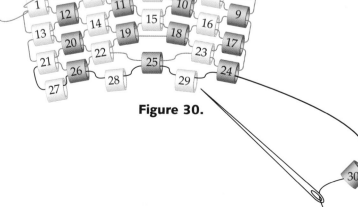

CAROL WILCOX WELLS
1776,
evening purse, 8 in. x 4¾ in. diameter (20.5 cm x 12 cm), peyote stitch, horizontal netting, Ultrasuede lining, satin cord, 11° cylinder seed beads, metal stand. PHOTO BY TIM BARNWELL.

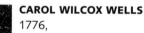

Figure 30.

Two-Drop Peyote

Two-drop peyote is done in the same way as regular peyote except that two beads are used in each step instead of one. Two-drop can be done either flat or tubular. The graphing process will be a little different; using two-drop peyote graph paper helps.

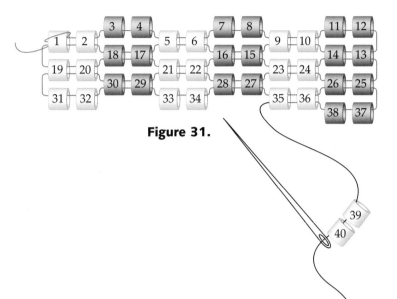

Figure 31.

Figure 31. String on 12 beads, pick up two more beads (#13 and #14), and stitch back through two beads (#10 and #9). Continue in this manner until the desired length is reached.

By using the same principle, you can weave three-drop, four-drop, or five-drop peyote. You can also move from two-drop to three-drop as a means of increasing and then decrease back to a single peyote.

LAURA GOLDBERG

Bird Hand Bag,

8 in. x 5 in. x 3 in.
(20.5 cm x 12.5 cm x 7.5 cm),
peyote and two-drop peyote
stitch, antique purse frame,
11° seed beads.

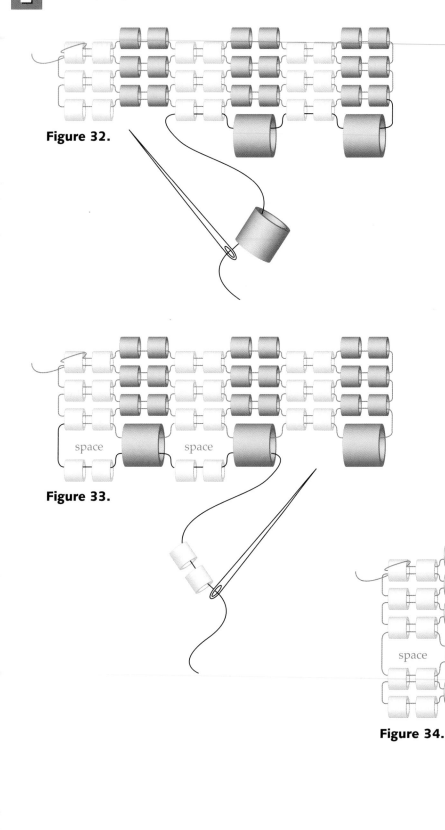

Figure 32.

Figure 33.

Figure 34.

TWO-DROP WITH 3.3 CYLINDER BEADS

Combining size 11° cylinder beads with the larger 3.3 cylinder beads creates a unique texture and look. Because the 3.3 bead is somewhat "fatter" than the size 11° bead, open spaces will occur around the 3.3 beads.

Figure 32. The 3.3 beads may be added at any time to a two-drop peyote piece. Here they are shown in row 7. Pick up one 3.3 bead and go through two 11° beads. Continue in this manner all the way across.

Figure 33. Now pick up two 11° beads and go through one 3.3 bead. The 11° beads may have a tendency to go inside the 3.3 beads, but the next row will put them back in their proper positions.

Figure 34. This illustration shows the addition of another row of 3.3s and the space created between them.

CAROL WILCOX WELLS Chatelaine Nouveau, *handmade synthetic suede belt with beaded purse, 6½ in. x 2¾ in. x ¾ in. (16.5 cm x 7 cm x 2 cm), peyote and two-drop peyote stitch, 11° cylinder seed beads, 3.3° cylinder seed beads, Bali silver, hematite, and other assorted beads.*

SINGLE PEYOTE COMBINED WITH TWO-DROP PEYOTE AND 3.3 CYLINDER BEADS

Figure 35. As this illustration shows, several techniques can be combined without leaving spaces between beads when using the larger 3.3 cylinder beads. There will be four threads passing through each 3.3 bead instead of the usual two.

Figure 35.

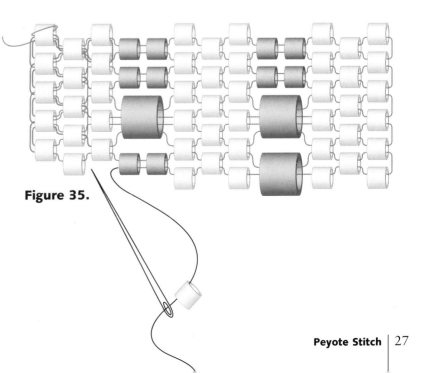

40/100
80
20

KATHLYN MOSS
Winter Blackberries,
*necklace, 11 in. x 6¼ in.
(28 cm x 15.5 cm),
circular peyote stitch,
11° seed beads.*

Circular Flat Peyote

Circular flat peyote takes a very linear stitch and transforms it into a radiating form. It is worked from the center outward, increasing as necessary to fill out a row. The increases should be equally spaced.

Try following the illustration using contrasting beads to get a feel for the process.

Figure 36. String three beads on the thread and slide them toward the end of the thread, leaving a 6-inch (15 cm) tail. Tie the beads into a ring, using a square knot, and pass the needle through bead #1.

For the next row, pick up two beads in each space. When you get to the end of a row, pass the needle through the first bead of the previous row and the first two beads of the row that you are on.

Each row will vary in the number of beads per stitch. As the piece widens, you will have to increase the number of beads per row. In row 3, each double set of beads from row 2 splits to form new spokes. There are now six stitches, rather than the three in the previous row.

The number of beads that form the initial ring can vary in number; you aren't limited to three. Try other variations on your own.

Figure 36.

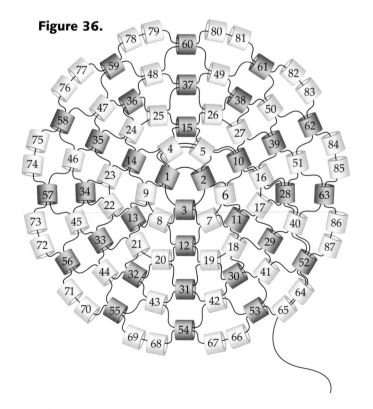

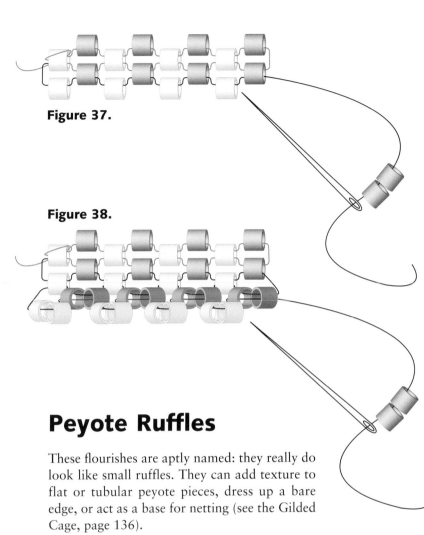

Figure 37.

Figure 38.

Peyote Ruffles

These flourishes are aptly named: they really do look like small ruffles. They can add texture to flat or tubular peyote pieces, dress up a bare edge, or act as a base for netting (see the Gilded Cage, page 136).

Figure 37. At the edge of a piece of peyote stitch, pick up two beads instead of one and pass the needle through one bead. Again, pick up two beads and go through one. Continue to do this all the way across the piece, pulling tightly as you go. The beads will not lie flat. Rather, they will bunch up, and it will be hard to see where you are going. To help find your way, use a striped pattern on your first ruffle, as shown in the illustration.

Figure 38. When working the next row, pick up two beads and go through two beads. Do this all the way across, being careful to go through the beads in the correct order. Keep the tension tight and continue with the next row, picking up two beads and going through two beads. It will take about six rows, counting on the diagonal, to achieve a good ruffle.

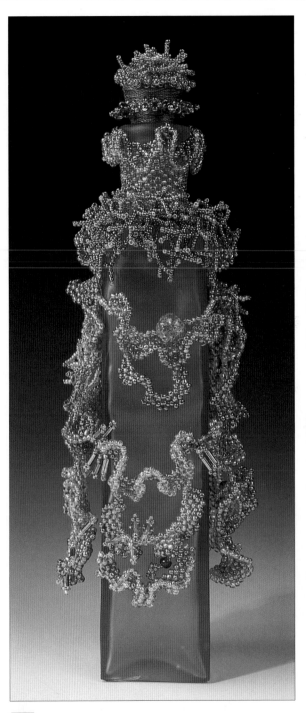

 TINA BLOOMENTHAL
Amber Waves, *beaded bottle,*
8 in. x 1½ in. x 1½ in. (20.5 cm x 4 cm x 4 cm),
peyote stitch and peyote ruffles embellished
with bugles, crystals, and assorted glass beads.

Peyote Spikes

Peyote spikes are somewhat like fringe, in that they extend away from the base of the work. The difference is that they can be added anywhere, not just along the bottom edge. They are made while weaving the base layer.

The spikes do not sit directly over a row of vertical beads but between two rows. They can be any length and made with any bead. The texture they provide is worth the effort to make them.

Figure 39. Pick up four beads; the first bead is the base bead. Pass the needle back through beads #3 and #2, bypassing the base bead. Weave into the next bead as if you were doing regular peyote stitch. Bead #1—the base bead—will go into its proper peyote position. Tighten the thread to align the spike.

Figure 40. As you add the next row, make sure that the base bead is being used as part of the regular peyote row. Continue with peyote stitch, adding as many spikes as you can handle. Make sure that the spikes stay on the right side of the piece while you are working. They have been known to migrate to the inside, and the only way to get them back is to take out to that point.

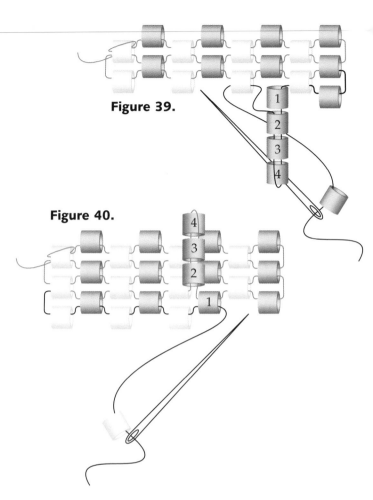

Figure 39.

Figure 40.

WENDY ELLSWORTH

Green Sea Form,

sculpture,
2¾ in. x 5 in. x 4¾ in.
(7 cm x 12.5 cm x 12 cm),
circular peyote stitch,
11° seed beads.
Collection of
Fleur Bresler

Figure 41.

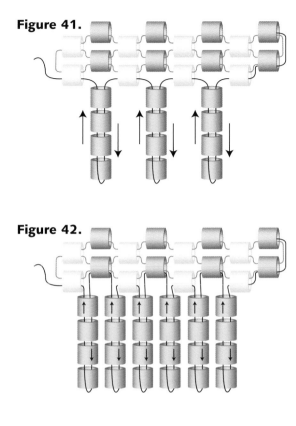

Figure 42.

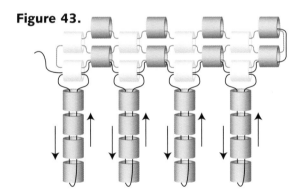

Figure 43.

Attaching Fringe

There are three ways to add fringe to peyote stitch: from protruding beads, between two vertical rows, and directly under a bead. The following illustrations will guide you through each of the techniques.

Figure 41. Fringe from protruding beads.

Figure 42. Fringe between two vertical rows.

Figure 43. Fringe directly under a bead.

 CAROL WILCOX WELLS
Past Midnight,
evening purse, 6 in. x 4½ in. diameter (15 cm x 11.5 cm), peyote stitch, horizontal netting, boned Ultrasuede lining, satin cord, 11° cylinder seed beads, metal stand. Collection of Dr. & Mrs. Reb Ivey

How to Read a Peyote Graph

You don't need a graph to weave peyote. You can simply pick up a needle and some beads and stitch away, changing color as you wish, increasing and decreasing as you choose.

Other times you'll want to work with a graph, to follow someone else's design or to work out a design of your own.

FLAT PEYOTE, EVEN-COUNT

Figure 44.

- Each rectangle represents one bead.
- Vertical rows are indicated by letters.
- Horizontal rows are indicated by numbers.
- The shaded beads show how to count on the diagonal.

Peyote stitch is a vertical brick pattern. The pattern forms when the third horizontal row of beads is added. The initial string of beads is actually rows 1 and 2 when counted on the diagonal.

Straight vertical lines can be made but not straight horizontal lines. Horizontal lines can be simulated by doing two or three rows of the same color. Curves can be implied by choosing beads within the shape desired (see the circle in the graph diagram).

Even-count peyote cannot accommodate a pattern that needs to be centered or a piece that needs to be decreased on the outside edges to a symmetrical point.

Looking at the diagram, notice that there is a protruding bead (L-1) on one outer edge and a recessed bead (A-2) on the other. When reading an even-count flat peyote graph, you must begin reading (adding beads) from the side that has the recessed bead on the outer edge. Work across, turn, and work back the other way.

Using a magnetic board and straightedge really helps in this process. Lay the graph on the board and place the magnetic straightedge along the row of beads that you are working on. After each row is finished, slide the straightedge down to the next row.

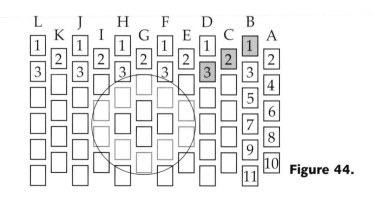

MARCIE STONE
Abalone Necklace, *8 in. x 7½ in. (20.5 cm x 19.5 cm), peyote stitch, abalone, garnets, fluorite, pearls, and assorted seed beads.*

Figure 44.

FLAT PEYOTE, ODD-COUNT

Figure 45. For odd-count flat peyote, both outer edges will be the same, having either protruding beads or recessed beads. When graphing, you must start with protruding beads on the outer edges. A pattern can be centered and a symmetrical point achieved with odd-count flat peyote.

When counting rows, you can count from one corner to another or diagonally down two adjacent rows.

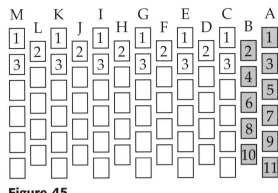

Figure 45.

CAROL WILCOX WELLS

Peonies and the Butterfly,

neck piece, 14½ in. x 8 in. (37 cm x 20.5 cm), peyote stitch, 11° cylinder seed beads, other assorted beads, and an antique French enamel button.

TUBULAR PEYOTE, EVEN-COUNT

Figure 46.

- Each rectangle represents one bead.
- Vertical rows are indicated by letters.
- Horizontal rows are indicated by numbers.
- The shaded beads show how to count on the diagonal and indicate the first bead of each horizontal row.

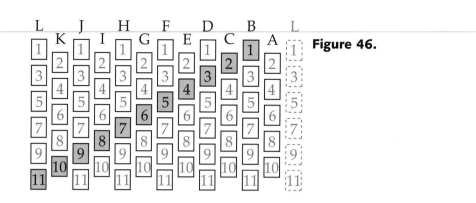

Figure 46.

While flat peyote is read from side to side, tubular peyote is read from the first bead of each horizontal row to the last bead of the same row, flowing around the piece. The first bead of each row will move one vertical row to the left, forming a diagonal line that will help you know where you are on the graph. Remember that the graph is flat and the work is three-dimensional. Vertical row L will be beside vertical row A in actuality.

If a pattern has a repeat, it must be equally divisible into the total number of beads originally strung on the thread.

NOTE: Because odd-count tubular peyote spirals, working out the pattern on one-dimensional graph paper is more confusing than helpful. Odd-count is best designed on the three-dimensional object as you work on it.

MARCIE STONE
Mobe Pearl Basket, 6½ in. x 7 in. diameter (16.5 cm x 18 cm), pine needle basket with peyote stitch surface embellishment, garnets, pearls, and assorted seed beads.

LINDSAY OBERMEYER
The Medicine Chest

sculpture, 10 in. x 12 in. x 4 in.
(25.5 cm x 30.5 cm x 10 cm),
peyote stitch worked around
over-the-counter bottles of
medicine, glass seed beads.

COURTESY OF MOBILIA GALLERY.

PHOTO BY JOHN PHELAN.

IN THE COLLECTION OF
MR. & MRS. ANDERSON.

project

Beaded Barrette

DESIGNER: **Wendy Ellsworth**

This snappy barrette is a very easy project. The pattern emerges quickly as the different colors of beads are added.

MATERIALS

- Beads

  Size 11° cylinder seed beads

  Black opaque hex cut: .5 gram

  White gold 22 kt hex cut: .5 gram

  Silver-lined dark red: 2 grams

- Beading thread, burgundy
- Beading needles, size 12
- French-style barrette,
  3 inches x ⅜ inch (7.5 x 1 cm)
- Leather strip, 2⅛ inch x ⅞ inch
  (6 x 2 cm)
- Leather glue
- Bead glue

TECHNIQUES USED

✓ Flat peyote, even-count

FINISHED SIZE

3 inches x ⅜ inch x ⅜ inch
  (7.5 x 1 x 1 cm)

INSTRUCTIONS

1. Following the graph, pick up 66 beads; these will become rows 1 and 2. Begin even-count flat peyote and continue until all beads have been added.

2. Remove the inner spring from the barrette. Apply leather glue to the wrong side of the leather strip and to the back side of the barrette, along its lower edge. Allow the glue to get tacky, then wrap the leather strip around the barrette, allowing the ends to meet on top of the barrette. Press into place and allow to dry.

3. Apply bead glue with a toothpick along the entire top of the leather-covered barrette. Carefully place the beaded strip on top of the barrette, allowing an equal overlap at both ends. Glue these ends to the underside of the barrette.

4. Sew the side edges of the beadwork together at both ends of the barrette.

5. Re-insert the inner spring into the barrette.

← *Start Here*

project

Small Beaded-Bead Lariat

DESIGNER: **Deneen Matson**

This elegant, feminine necklace is composed of beads made from beads. The beads are simple to make and the varieties endless.

MATERIALS

- Beads

  Size 11° cylinder seed beads:
    Dark bronze iridescent: 10 grams
    Matte copper: 10 grams

- Beading thread, brown
- Beading needles, size 12

TECHNIQUES USED

✓ Flat peyote, even-count
✓ Flat peyote, odd-count
✓ Surface embellishment

FINISHED SIZE

32 inches (81.5 cm) long

INSTRUCTIONS

MAKING THE BEADS

1. For each beaded bead, weave a piece of flat peyote seven or 10 beads wide and eight to 10 beads deep, counting on the diagonal. See Figure 1. Make 32 pieces.

2. Roll each flat piece into a tube so that the edges interlock and weave them together.

3. To give a bead extra dimension, add a narrow band of peyote embellishment to its surface. See Figure 2. Make the band long enough to wrap around the base bead. Fit its interlocking ends together and weave them securely. Vary the width, color, and placement of these surface bands.

On the necklace shown, there are seven dark bronze iridescent beads that are 10 beads wide and 8 beads deep; 21 matte copper beads that are 10 beads wide and 8 beads deep; and four multi-colored beaded beads that are seven beads wide and 10 beads deep.

STRINGING THE NECKLACE

4. Using a doubled thread 36 inches (91.5 cm) long, weave into one of the larger beads and anchor the thread. Exit through the center end of that bead.

5. String on nine single beads, alternating the two colors, then a beaded bead. Continue with this pattern until all of the beaded beads have been used.

6. Tie off the thread in the last beaded bead and add a few fringes to both ends of the necklace.

Figure 1.

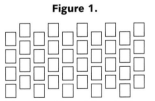

10 beads wide x 8 beads deep

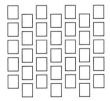

7 beads wide x 10 beads deep

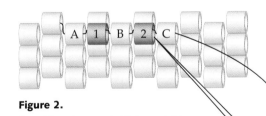

Figure 2.

To add surface embellishment (shown here as dark beads), have the needle exit bead A. Pick up bead 1 and go into bead B. Pick up bead 2 and go into bead C. Now pick up bead 3, turn, and go into bead 2. You are now set to do a four-bead-wide strip around the base bead.

Electric Blues Amulet Purse

DESIGNER: **Kathy Robin**

The popularity of beaded amulet purses is matched only by the variety of shapes, colors, and patterns in which they appear. An interesting feature of this one is that it has two "windows" woven into the body and front flap of the purse.

MATERIALS

- Beads
  Size 11° cylinder seed beads
      Black opaque hex cut: 7.5 grams
      Semi-matte silver-lined medium
          blue: 30 grams
  Purse Accent Beads
      8 mm Bali silver bugles: 2
      3 mm black crystals: 4
      4 mm black bicone crystals: 2
      3 mm silver square cut: 6
      7 mm Bali silver cylinder: 1
  Strap Accent Beads
      4 mm black bicone crystals: 10
      4 mm Bali silver: 4
  Fringe Beads
  Assorted black & silver beads

- Beading thread, navy
- Beading needles, size 12
- Cardboard tube

TECHNIQUES USED

✓ Tubular peyote, even-count
✓ Flat Peyote, odd-count
  and even-count
✓ Decreasing outside edges
✓ Fringe

FINISHED SIZE

6 inches x 2 inches x ¼ inch
  (15 x 5 x .5 cm)

Figure 1.

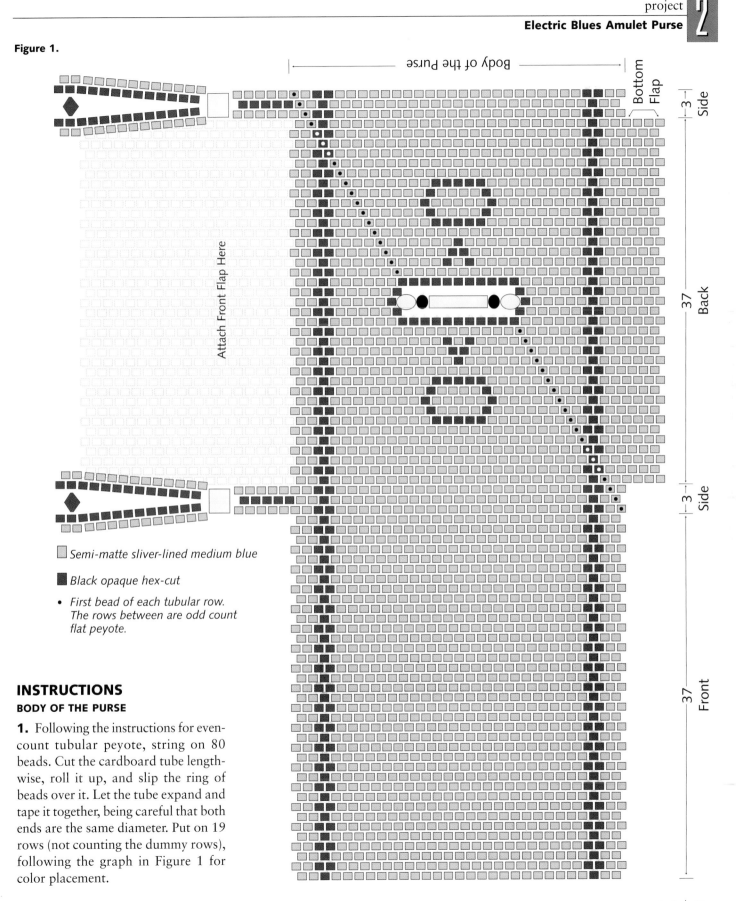

Semi-matte sliver-lined medium blue

Black opaque hex-cut

• First bead of each tubular row. The rows between are odd count flat peyote.

INSTRUCTIONS
BODY OF THE PURSE

1. Following the instructions for even-count tubular peyote, string on 80 beads. Cut the cardboard tube length-wise, roll it up, and slip the ring of beads over it. Let the tube expand and tape it together, being careful that both ends are the same diameter. Put on 19 rows (not counting the dummy rows), following the graph in Figure 1 for color placement.

2. Row 20 is where the formation of the window begins. At this point you will begin odd-count flat peyote on the tube. Instead of going around and around the tube, you will turn when you get to the window and go the other way. When you reach the window on the other side, you'll reverse again. Do this through row 40, keeping the window edges as straight as you can.

3. At the end of row 41, you will be coming out of the bottom right black bead in the window frame. Pick up three black beads and go into the bottom left black bead in the window frame. Continue around, doing tubular peyote, until you get to the three black beads. Pass the needle through all three and finish the row.

4. When you reach the black beads again, in row 42, pass through the middle one only just as you would while doing a regular row. This will set the three black beads into the correct position. Finish the rest of the body of the purse.

BOTTOM FLAP

5. Looking at the graph for placement and size, bead the bottom flap, using odd-count flat peyote. Fold the bottom flap toward the front, bypassing the three vertical rows that make up each side of the purse. Weave the interlocking beads together; see Figure 2.

6. Stitch the bottom to the sides, as shown in Figure 3. Catch the protruding beads first, then reverse direction and catch the recessed beads.

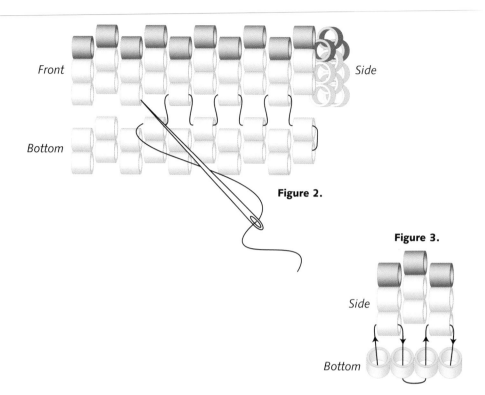

Front

Side

Bottom

Figure 2.

Figure 3.

Side

Bottom

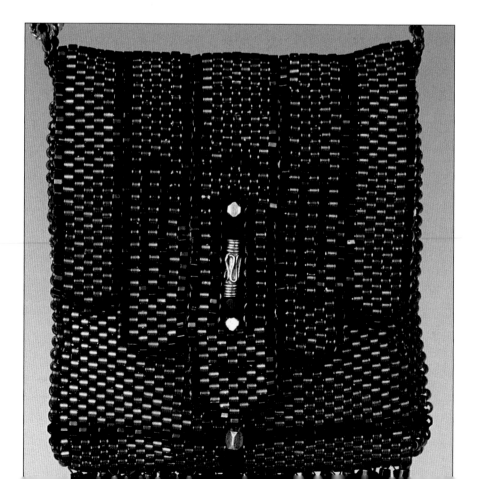

FRONT FLAP

7. The front flap is done in odd-count flat peyote. It has a window and decreases on the outside edges. If you started with three dummy rows, remove them now before adding the front flap. Now begin the flap on the upper back side, following the graph in Figure 4.

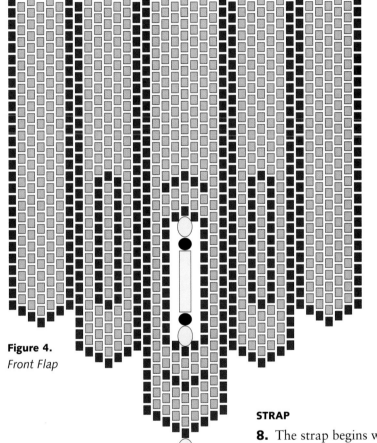

Figure 4.
Front Flap

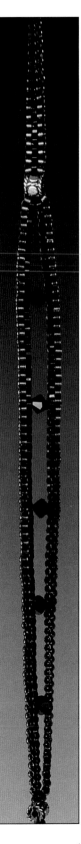

Figure 5.
Strap

STRAP

8. The strap begins with 10 rows of odd-count flat peyote. See the graph in Figure 5. A 4 mm Bali silver cylinder is added and should be reinforced by weaving through it several times. Now add another needle and thread and weave up through the large silver bead. One needle should be coming out from the right and one from the left.

9. Using one needle, begin an even-count flat peyote strip two beads wide and 24 beads long. Do the same with the other needle. Now pick up a crystal and pass both needles through it from opposite sides; continue the strap. Add four more crystals, then another 4 mm silver cylinder. At this point, switch back to the three-bead-wide peyote section. Do this for 20 inches (51 cm) and then revert to the split with crystals section. Attach the strap to the body of the purse, taking care not to twist it.

FRINGE

The purse has three rows of fringe that hang equally spaced from the bottom of the purse. See Figures 6, 7, and 8 for beads and length.

10. Now add the beads to the back and front flap windows. And don't forget the single fringe on the front flap.

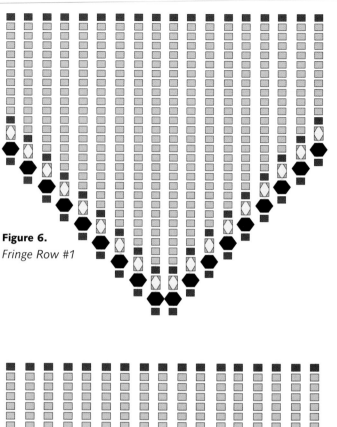

Figure 6.
Fringe Row #1

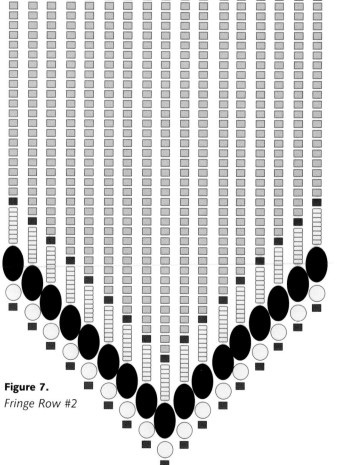

Figure 7.
Fringe Row #2

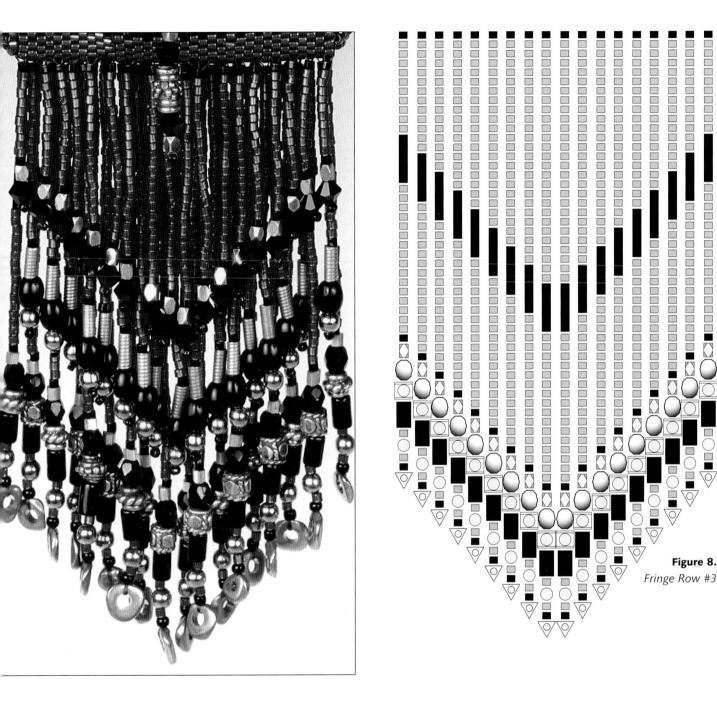

Figure 8.
Fringe Row #3

Maui Evening Purse

DESIGNER: **Catherine Harris**

*With its repeating patterns and subtle texture, this purse will provide
hours of pleasure in the weaving and generations of pleasure in the wearing.*

MATERIALS

- Beads
  Size 11° seed beads
    Blue iris: 2 grams
    Red gold luster: 5 grams
    Dark green opaque luster: 10 grams
    Cream opaque luster: 16 grams
    Matte green: 20 grams
    Matte cream: 31 grams
    Antique gold: 37 grams
  Accent beads
    Small green pear-shaped beads: 2
    Large green teardrop beads: 2
    9 mm cream opaque luster bugles: 6

- Beading thread, sand, 2 bobbins
- Beading needles, size 12
- 5 feet (2 m) of antique gold cord, for the strap
- Cardboard tube cut from 26-ounce (750 g) container of table salt

TECHNIQUES USED

✓ Tubular peyote, even-count
✓ Flat Peyote, odd-count
✓ Decreasing outside edges

FINISHED SIZE

5 x 4½ x ½ inch
  (12.5 x 11.5 x 1.5 cm)

INSTRUCTIONS

BODY OF THE PURSE

The body of the purse is worked in tubular peyote, even-count, around the cardboard tube. The flap and bottom are done in odd-count flat peyote.

Note that the graph shown for the body of the purse is half of the pattern needed to complete the design. Each horizontal row of tubular peyote should be done twice. The flat-peyote bottom shown on the graph should be woven only once.

1. String 144 beads on a 3-foot (.9 m) length of thread. Tie in a circle, leaving a space 7 beads wide. Place the ring of beads over the support. If needed, you can enlarge the tube by wrapping paper around it for a snug fit.

2. Weave three dummy rows, which will be removed later. The bead ring is rows 1 and 2. Stitch row 3 and then start the pattern, following the graph in Figure 1, starting in the upper right corner.

3. Work the pattern from top to bottom, adding beads from right to left. The dots indicate the first bead of each row.

BOTTOM FLAP

4. Following the graph in Figure 1 for placement and size, bead the bottom flap, using odd-count flat peyote.

5. Fold the bottom flap toward the front, bypassing the five vertical rows that make up each side of the purse. Weave the interlocking beads together. See Figure 2.

6. Stitch the bottom to the sides as shown in Figure 3. Catch the protruding beads first, then reverse direction and catch the recessed beads.

FRONT FLAP

The front flap is done in odd-count flat peyote and decreases on the outside edges.

7. Remove the three false rows at the top of the purse. Begin the flap on the upper back side following the graph in Figure 4. Make sure that it is in alignment with the bottom flap.

SIDE EMBELLISHMENT

8. Six loops of beads in varying lengths are added to each side of the purse, using accent beads and 11° seed beads.

Five beads make up each side of the body. Bring the needle out of the middle, top bead on one side of the purse. Add two loops to that bead and two loops to each of the next two beads directly under the middle bead. Add three fringes with bugles under the loops. Add embellishment to the other side.

STRAP

The strap is made from the gold cord and is attached to the inside of the purse at the sides, by peyote tubes. Have the cording before you make the tubes.

The tube is formed inside the body of the purse by using the three middle vertical rows that make up the side. See the upper left corner of the graph in Figure 1; the black dots indicate the beads used.

9. Pass the needle through the top three beads marked with black dots. String enough beads on the thread to form a snug ring around the cord. Remove the cord. Pass the needle back through the three middle beads to form a circle; see Figure 5. Do tubular peyote stitch using three beads from the side of the bag each time a row is stitched. This attaches the tube all the way down the inside of the purse. Work 18 rows and tie off.

10. Tightly wrap the ends of the cord with the clear tape. Pass the cord through to the bottom of the tube and anchor in place by stitching through the beaded tube and cord. Do this several times to secure. Use a regular sewing needle for this step.

NOTE: Use a different thread to attach the cord than the one used for the beaded tube. If the cord needs replacing, the beaded tube won't unravel when it is taken out.

do this one column

Figure 1.

Graph for half of the purse body and all of the bottom flap

Side

Body of Purse

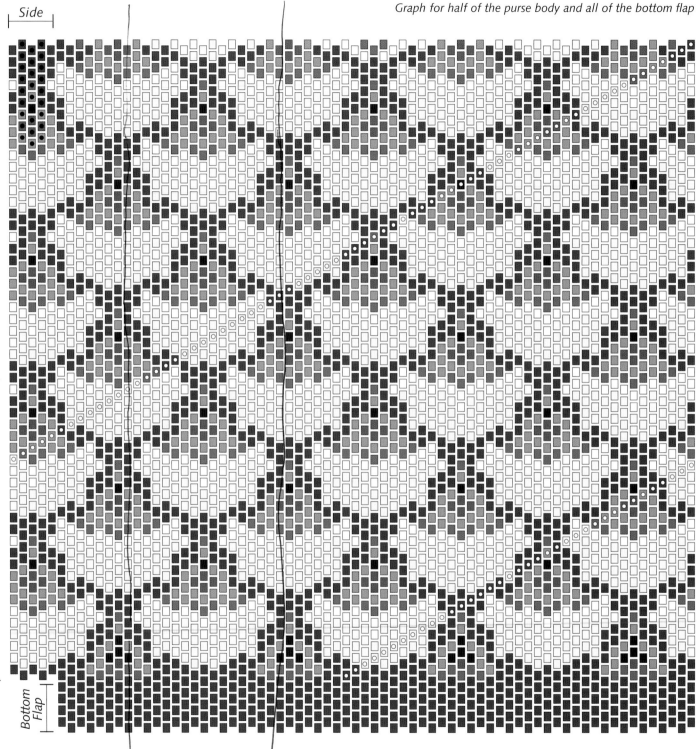

Bottom Flap

○ *First Bead of Each Row*
□ *Pale Cream*
□ *Cream*
■ *Bronze*
■ *Rose*
■ *Blue Iris*
■ *Matte Green*
■ *Green Iris*

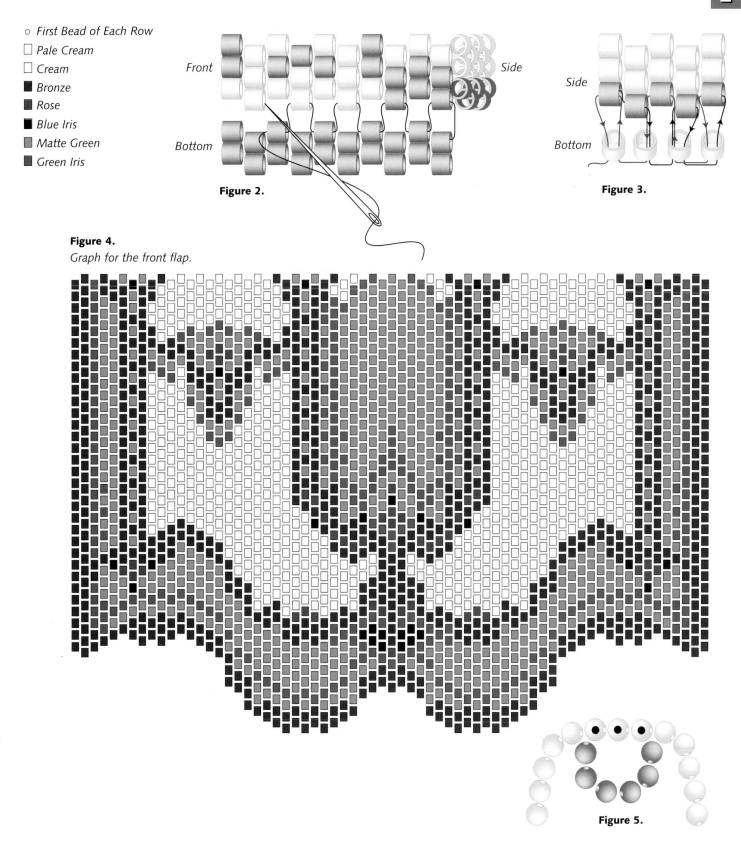

Front

Side

Figure 2.

Side

Bottom

Figure 3.

Bottom

Figure 4.
Graph for the front flap.

Figure 5.

project

Two-Carrot Earrings

DESIGNER: **Liz Manfredini**

These tubular peyote earrings are fun to make and delightful to wear. The green leaves are made from a looped version of branched fringe.

MATERIALS

- Beads
  Size 11° seed beads
    Orange: 8 grams
    Green: 6 grams

- Beading thread, orange and green
- Beading needles, size 12
- Pair of french ear wires
- 2 1½-inch (4 cm) eye pins
- Orange felt

TECHNIQUES USED

✓ Tubular peyote, even-count
✓ Decreasing
✓ Looped branch fringe

FINISHED SIZE

2¾ x ½ inch (7 x 1.5 cm)

INSTRUCTIONS

CARROT

1. Using the pattern in Figure 1, cut a pennant shape out of the orange felt. Starting with the short end A, roll the felt up to side B, keeping the top edge even.

2. Wrap the felt with orange thread until a carrot cone shape is formed. It will be fairly compact when you are through.

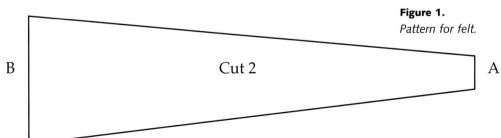

B   Cut 2   A

Figure 1.
Pattern for felt.

3. Start even-count tubular peyote with 20 orange beads. Position them about ¼ inch (.5 cm) from the top of the felt carrot. The bottom of the carrot will be done first, decreasing as follows.

> **Rows 1 through 4:** 10 beads
>
> **Row 5:** 8 beads
>
> **Row 6:** 6 beads
>
> **Row 7:** 4 beads
>
> **Row 8:** 4 beads and close

The number of beads may vary according to the size of the carrot base.

4. Weave the thread back up to the initial row and stitch the top of the carrot, decreasing when necessary to fit around the felt base.

LEAVES

Start with a heavier, perhaps doubled thread for this part, because you will want stiffness in the leaves.

5. Secure the thread by going back and forth through the carrot base and pull up through the top. Add 18 green beads. Loop down and pass the needle through bead #11. Come out of bead #10 and pick up seven beads; pass the needle through beads #9 and #8. Repeat until you have four leaves on the stalk and five beads left on the bottom. See Figure 2.

6. Bring the thread through the last five beads and down into the carrot. Come

out the side somewhere and pull it tight. Secure the thread and go back up through the top of the carrot and add another set of leaves. Repeat until there are seven sets of leaves.

FINDINGS

7. File the end of the eye pin to a point for easier insertion into the carrot. Then attach the french earring wire to the eye pin. Add a dab of glue to the eye pin post and insert into the center of the top of the carrot.

8. Complete the other earring.

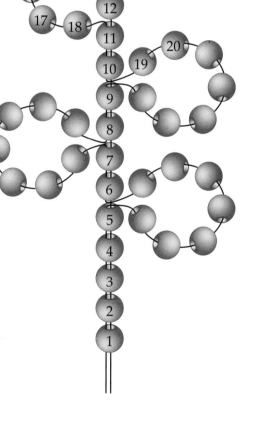

Figure 2.
Carrot Leaves

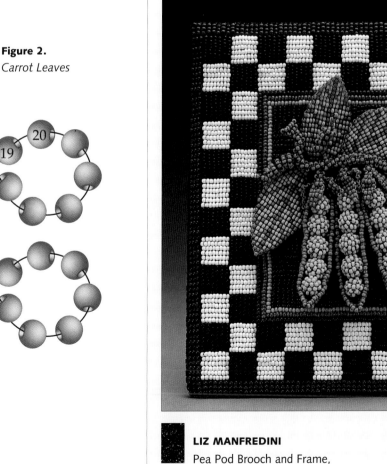

LIZ MANFREDINI
Pea Pod Brooch and Frame,
6½ in. x 5¾ in. x 1 in. (16.5 cm x 14.5 cm x 2.5 cm), peyote stitch (peas, pod, and stem), square stitch (leaves), bead embroidery (frame), 11° seed beads. PHOTO: Joe Manfredini

Mortimer the Figure Pin

DESIGNER: **Merri Beth Hill**

Browsing at a craft show, Merri Beth Hill stumbled upon an antique Zuni figure stitched around a rabbit's foot. It had a peyote stitch head and bead fringe fingers; its feet were two rabbit-foot toes with the hair still intact. Entranced, she set about re-creating the figure—without the stiff interior, and making use of the great button heads and metal hands now available.

MATERIALS

- Beads

  Size 11° seed beads in 2 colors (one for pants and one for shirt): about 6 grams

  2 trim beads for hands

  2 trim beads for feet

- Face button
- Beading thread
- Beading needles, size 12
- Long tapestry needle
- 2-inch (5 cm) piece of 16-gauge wire
- 2-inch (5 cm) piece of leather or synthetic suede
- 1-inch (2.5 cm) bar pin finding
- Glue
- Needle-nose pliers

TECHNIQUES USED

✓ Tubular peyote, odd-count
✓ Decreasing
✓ Fringe

FINISHED SIZE

4 inches x 1½ inches x ¼ inch (10 x 4 x .5 cm)

PREVIEW

In constructing this figure, four peyote stitch cylinders are made—two for the arms and two for the legs. The legs are made first, then joined and expanded into one larger cylinder, the torso. The arms are added to the torso much like a circular knit sweater, decreasing at the top to form the neckline. A flexible "skeleton" thread is strung through the inside of the beaded "suit" to join the hands and feet. The head and pin back complete the construction.

INSTRUCTIONS

1. Start with a single 30-inch (76 cm) length of thread and the pant beads. Begin at the bottom of the leg with a circle of nine beads and work odd-count tubular peyote for a depth of 28 rows, counting on the diagonal. See Figure 1. Make two of these for the legs.

2. Using the beads for the shirt, make the arms in the same manner as the legs, except shorter--only 20 beads deep. See Figure 2. Leave a long tail of thread at the start of the arms so that a contrasting row of beads can be added for a cuff and adjustment of beads around the hands.

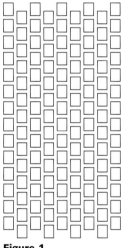

Figure 1.
*Graph for Pant/Legs
Make 2*

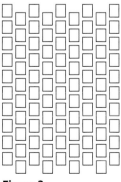

Figure 2.
Graph for Arms Make 2

NOTE: Leave the lengths of thread loose and hanging at the tops of the legs and arms; you'll use them to close the crotch and armpit gaps after the body/suit beading is finished. The thread from the top of one leg joins the two legs together and starts the torso. The continuing torso thread joins the arms to the torso.

3. To join the two legs, continue beading with one of the top of the leg threads, starting where your 28th row finished, by adding one bead between the two legs and continuing to the next stitch in the top of the second leg. When you are nearly around the second leg, come out the next to the last bead in the ring; this time, add three beads before continuing peyote stitch back into the first leg. See Figure 3. The new single ring of beads should now have a count of 19.

4. Proceed to build the top on the pants until you have beaded 12 rows, counting on the diagonal, up from where the legs joined.

Figure 3.
Joining legs to form top of pants/torso.

Add 3 beads at the back and 1 at the front.

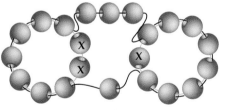

Skip the beads marked with an X at center tops of legs to form a new ring of 19.

Figure 4.
Joining arms to torso.

Add one bead at each side/front and each side/back at the body/sleeve junction for a total of 4 beads added.

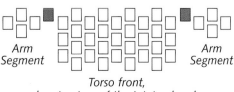

*Arm
Segment*

*Arm
Segment*

*Torso front,
showing two of the joining beads.*

5. Start the shirt/arm color at the side and add 12 rows, counting on the diagonal. It is now time to join the arms.

NOTE: Each arm will be joined at the front and back of the torso by adding a bead between the two pieces, for a total of four beads added. You will not go through all of the beads in the arm circles; one or two adjacent beads in the armpit will be excluded from the shoulder circle.

6. With the needle attached to an arm thread, add three beads in normal peyote fashion around the top of the arm. Now pick up a bead and join it to the torso. Do four more stitches and add another joining bead. Continue around, adding two more joining beads on the back. See Figure 4. After both arms are attached, there should be a circle of 35 beads. Do one complete row around the circle, then snug up the tension and knot the thread at the center back to the previous row thread to hold the arm joins in place.

7. The next circular row will decrease four times—once at the front and once at the back on each side, just above where the arm and torso join. See Figure 5. Decrease again on the next row in the same way. Work one more row around the neck; do not decrease. Knot the thread at the back and add a new thread for the fringe at the neckline.

NOTE: Put less collar fringe on the back than on the front, so that the pin will lie flatter.

Figure 5.
Detail of shoulder decrease.

Decrease above each of the four juncture beads.

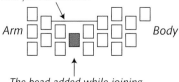

Arm

Body

The bead added while joining the arm to the body.

8. For the back, each fringe is put on between the two "protruding" beads. On the front, put a fringe between, and on top of, the "protruding" beads to suit your own taste.

9. To string the hands and feet together, use a long, large-eyed needle and small pliers to grasp and feed the thread through the beaded suit. Cut a piece of thread about 30 inches (76 cm) long. Fold it in half and loop it through the top of one of the foot beads. Run the two ends up through one leg and out of the neck hole.

10. Take one of the threads and feed it down the opposite arm. Loop it through a hand bead, back up the inside of the arm, and out again at the neck. Carefully adjust the tension so the hand and foot both hang freely without puckering the beadwork. Tie off just below the fringe on the back.

11. Next take the unused half of the skeleton thread and feed it down the remaining leg. Add the second foot, then run the thread back into the body and out the remaining armhole. Add the second hand and bring the thread out at the neck. Adjust the tension and secure. See Figure 6.

12. Cut a 2-inch (5 cm) piece of wire. Thread it through the shank of the face button twice and bend the ends into loops. See Figure 7. If desired, make a beaded crown. Position and glue it on the back of the button; let dry. Apply a blob of glue to the back of the button and cover the button and the wires with a piece of suede or leather, allowing the two wire loops to extend downward for the neck. Let dry thoroughly before adding to the body.

NOTE: It is easier to trim the edge of the leather after the glue dries. You can cut it into decorative shapes if you like.

13. To attach the head, cut a 20-inch (51 cm) piece of thread and double it. Loop and knot through the two rounded wires at the bottom of the neck. Thread a large-eyed needle with both threads and insert the needle down and through the neck hole, exiting between beads through the center back of the suit, about ½ inch (1.5 cm) down from the neck hole. Gently pull downward until the head rests on the shoulders/fringe and none of the neck wire shows. Thread a beading needle with the individual ends of the thread and go through a few of the back beads, knotting to secure the head position.

14. Sew the bar pin onto the center of the back vertically, using the ends of the head threads. The top of the pin should be attached just below the neck fringe. While you are stitching on the pin, tack the neck wire to the back of the suit, being careful not to catch the suit front. For a tidy finish, do a buttonhole stitch over the pin back.

15. Close up the top around the neck. Secure the embellishment of your choice on the front of the suit, and add a row of contrasting beads for sleeve cuffs. Tie off any loose threads.

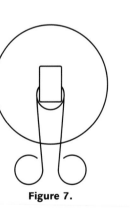

Figure 6.
String hands and feet using a 30-inch (76 cm.) thread, doubled.

Figure 7.

ANOTHER VERSION OF MORTIMER PIN,

woven by Carol Wilcox Wells, using metal beads for hands and feet. The porcelain face button was designed by Jane Guerber and produced by Howard Newcomb of Portland, Oregon.

project

Double Mandala Earrings

DESIGNER: **Carol Wilcox Wells**

This easy project provides prompt (if not instant) gratification, as well as the opportunity to practice a new technique.

MATERIALS

- Beads

  Size 11° seed beads

    Matte light amethyst iridescent: 2 grams

    Metallic burgundy: 8 grams

  Trim Beads

    4 mm dark amethyst iridescent crystals: 26

- Beading thread, burgundy
- Beading needles, size 12
- 2-inch (5 cm) square of synthetic suede, burgundy
- Pair of 10 mm bullet post earring findings
- Two-part epoxy

TECHNIQUES USED

✓ Peyote, circular flat

✓ Fringe

✓ Surface embellishment

FINISHED SIZE

2½ x 1 inch (6.5 x 2.5 cm)

INSTRUCTIONS

1. Follow the graph in Figure 1 for the base of the earring. For the dark colored beads, use the metallic burgundy; for the light beads, use the light amethyst. When the base is finished, secure the thread. If it is still fairly long, weave into position to begin the surface embellishment.

2. Figure 2 shows the placement of the second layer of beads. Begin by weaving to bead #68; see Figure 1. Pass the needle through bead #68, pick up a dark bead, and go through bead #69. Pick up five beads, alternating dark and light, and pass through bead #72. Repeat this pattern all the way around until you reach the beginning. Weave through beads #68, #69, #55, and #44.

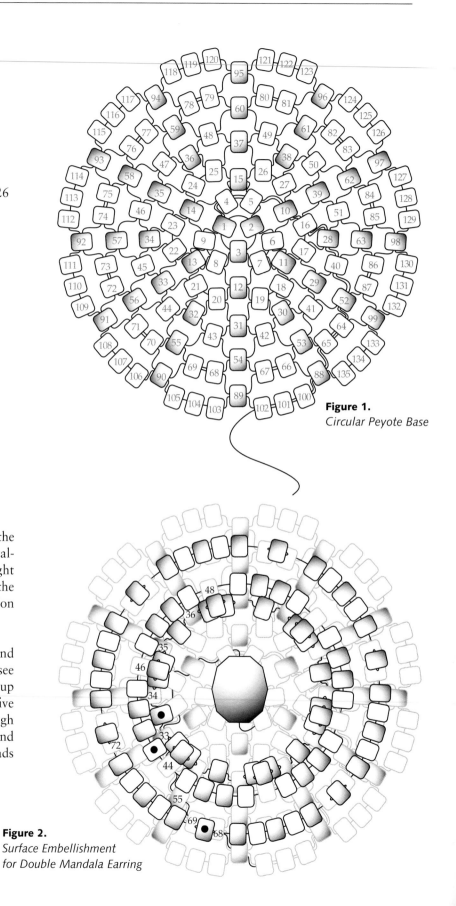

Figure 1.
Circular Peyote Base

Figure 2.
*Surface Embellishment
for Double Mandala Earring*

3. Pick up four beads—light, dark, dark, light—and pass the needle through bead #46. Repeat all the way around.

4. Weave to bead #33, add a dark bead, and go into #34. Pick up three dark beads and go into bead #35. Continue adding beads in this manner until you finish the row.

5. Weave to the center and add a 4 mm crystal. Tie off the thread.

6. The fringe is attached to the base and to the surface embellishment. Follow Figure 3 for placement and size.

7. Glue the earring post to the back of the earring and let dry.

8. Cut a ¾-inch-diameter (2 cm) circle out of burgundy suede, put a pin hole in the center, and slide it over the earring post. Check the position, then glue into place and let dry.

9. Make the other earring.

Figure 3.
Fringe

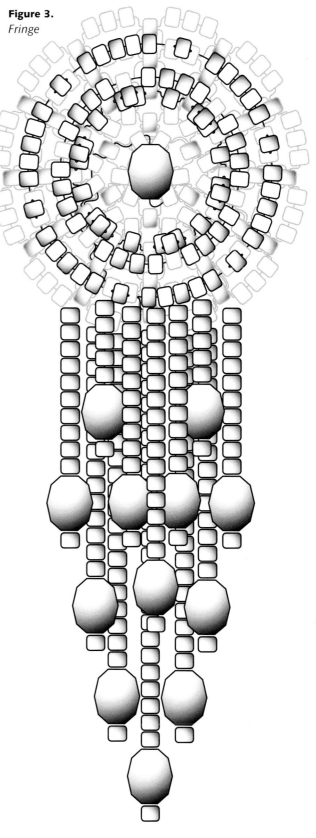

Hollow Beaded Bead with Tubular Necklace

DESIGNER: **Carol Wilcox Wells**

The Hollow Beaded Bead began as a way to teach beginning peyote students how to increase and decrease within a tubular form. After making their samples, they would look at me and ask, "Why would anyone want to do this?" I would share at length all of the applications and possibilities; they would continue to look. So I thought up a way to turn their instructional samples into wearable art.

MATERIALS

- Beads

  Size 11° cylinder seed beads

  Lined light violet iridescent:
  7.5 grams

  Matte metallic yellow gold
  22kt: 5 grams

  Matte metallic white gold
  22kt: 7.5 grams

  Size 15° round seed beads,
  metallic copper: 18 grams

  4 mm Czech fire-polished
  beads, metallic bronze: 2

- Beading thread, brown
  and sand

- Beading needles, size 12

- Gold box clasp, ⅜-inch
  (1 cm) square

- Dowel, 5 inches x ³⁄₁₆ inch
  (12.5 cm x 6 mm)

- Dowel, 5 inches x ⁷⁄₁₆ inch
  (1.5 cm)

TECHNIQUES USED

✓ Tubular peyote, even-count

✓ Increasing within (two-drop and three-drop)

✓ Decreasing within (single and two-drop)

✓ Peyote ruffles

NECKLACE COMPONENTS

1 hollow beaded bead

20-inch (51 cm) beaded necklace

FINISHED SIZE

Bead: 2¼ inch x 1 inch diameter (6 x 1.5 cm)

Necklace: 20 inches x ¼ inch diameter (51 x .5 cm)

Figure 1.

← *Start Here*

☐ *Matte metallic white gold 22kt*
▨ *Matte metallic yellow gold 22kt*
■ *Lined light violet iridescent*
● *First Bead/Beads of Each Row*

NOTE:

*This peyote graph may look
different from the ones that
you are used to seeing, because
it shows the increases and
decreases.*

*To follow this graph, lay
a straightedge across the page
and line up the boxes in the
first row. As you finish a row,
slide the straightedge down
and continue with the next
row just as you would with a
regular graph. The open
spaces between vertical rows
on the graph will not show in
the actual beadwork.*

Hollow Beaded Bead with Tubular Necklace

INSTRUCTIONS

THE BEAD

1. Thread the needle and string on 28 beads, following the graph in Figure 1. Tie into a ring, leaving no thread space, and slide onto the large dowel. This is the form for the beaded bead.

2. Now make the bead, working in even-count tubular peyote, increasing and decreasing as shown on the graph. Keep the tension fairly tight so that when the dowel is removed, you will have a three-dimensional form.

3. When you have finished with the graph, put peyote ruffles on both ends of the bead, using 15° seed beads.

NECKLACE

This tubular necklace is made with 15° seed beads and cylinder seed beads. It is 14 beads around and 20 inches (51 cm) long.

4. Make the necklace in even-count tubular peyote, following the graph in Figure 2. Use the small dowel as a form for easier handling at the start. After you've woven about 1 inch (2.5 cm), remove the dowel and continue to weave. Keep the tension tight.

5. When the desired length is reached, decrease to close up the ends. Knot to secure. Coming from the center of one of the ends, pick up a 15° bead and a 4 mm bead; attach them to one side of the clasp. Reinforces several times. Repeat on the other end.

6. Slide the hollow beaded bead onto the tubular necklace.

Figure 2.

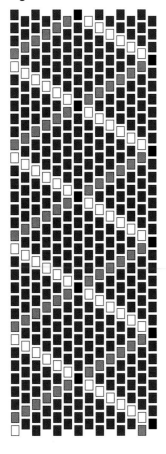

15° SEED BEAD

■ *copper*

11° CYLINDER SEED BEADS

■ *Matte metallic yellow gold 22 kt*

□ *Matte metallic white gold 22 kt*

▨ *Lined light violet iridescent*

Black and Gold Beaded-Bead Necklace

DESIGNER: **JoAnn Baumann**

This handsome necklace is much easier to make than the lengthy instructions might imply. There are many parts, but each is simple and fun to construct.

MATERIALS

- Beads

  21 wooden beads of varying sizes, graduated from 12 mm to 22 mm

  Size 11° seed beads
  Matte black: approx. 85 grams
  Gold: approx. 50 grams

  Size 15° seed beads, gold: approx. 3 grams.

- Beading thread, black
- Beading needles, size 12
- Black acrylic paint
- Black cording: approx. 36 inches (91.5 cm), depending on size and number of beads used

TECHNIQUES USED

✓ Tubular peyote (even-count) in single, two-drop, and three drop

✓ Increasing within a piece

✓ Decreasing within a piece

✓ Peyote ruffle

✓ Surface embellishment

NECKLACE COMPONENTS

21 beaded wooden beads

20 beaded spacer beads

Beaded tube

Black cording

FINISHED SIZE

14 inches x 1 inch (35.5 cm x 2.5 cm)

INSTRUCTIONS

1. Paint the wooden beads with the acrylic paint and let dry.

2. Bead the painted wooden beads. Directions for two of the beads follow. Work the remaining beads to suit your fancy.

MELON BEAD

This three-drop, even-count, tubular peyote bead is two beads out from the center on each side.

3. Thread the needle with a single 3-foot (.9 m) strand of thread. String on 42 beads, alternating 3 black and 3 gold. This is the center row. Pass the needle through all the beads again to form a circle, and tie a knot to secure. Slide this ring of beads to the center of a round, 20 mm painted wooden bead. The fit will be snug. Secure this row of beads to the center of the wooden bead at four points to hold them in place. See Figure 1.

4. Using three-drop peyote, begin beading down from the center row to the bottom of the wooden bead. As the wooden bead curves inward, you will have to decrease the number of beads in each row. This is done by going from three-drop to two-drop to single peyote.

5. When you have finished with one side, weave back through the beads to the center row and begin the other side. Have the thread coming out of three gold beads, with black beads to the left.

6. When you have woven the second half of the bead, sew through the last row again to secure it and tie off the thread.

PATTERN FOR MELON BEAD

First Half

Center row (rows 1 & 2 counting on the diagonal): 3 black, 3 gold.

Row 3: three-drop peyote, black.

Row 4: three-drop peyote, gold.

Row 5: three-drop peyote, black.

Row 6: three-drop peyote, gold.

Row 7: alternate two-drop & three-drop, black.

Row 8: alternate two-drop & three-drop, gold.

Row 9: two-drop, black.

Row 10: two-drop, gold.

Row 11: alternate single & two-drop, black.

Row 12: alternate single & two-drop, gold.

Row 13: single peyote, black.

Row 14: single peyote, gold.

Second Half

Row 3a: three-drop peyote, gold.

Row 4a: three-drop peyote, black.

Row 5a: three-drop peyote, gold.

Row 6a: three-drop peyote, black.

Row 7a: alternate three-drop & two-drop, gold.

Row 8a: alternate three-drop & two-drop, black.

Row 9a: two-drop, gold.

Row 10a: two-drop, black.

Row 11a: alternate two-drop & single, gold.

Row 12a: alternate two-drop & single, black.

Row 13a: single peyote, gold.

Row 14a: single peyote, black.

NOTE: Each bead that you make may vary, so the exact count may vary by a bead or two, but the overall effect should still be the same.

Figure 1.

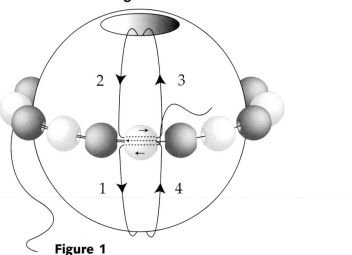

Figure 1

Slide the ring of seed beads onto the wooden bead. Pass the needle through a seed bead, going to the left. Go down (1) and up through the center of the wooden bead, then back down (2) to the same seed bead, passing through it to the right. Now go up (3) and back down through the wooden bead, up (4) and through the seed bead to the left. Keeping these threads tight, take the needle through the seed beads till you're a quarter of the way around the wooden bead and secure again. Repeat twice more.

CHEVRON BEAD

This even-count tubular peyote bead is the farthest bead back on each side of the necklace.

7. Thread the needle with a single 3-foot (.9 m) strand of thread. String on 32 beads, alternating 2 black and 2 gold. This is the center row. Pass the needle through all the beads again to form a circle and tie a knot to secure. Slide this ring of beads to the center of an oval (13 mm x 19 mm) painted wooden bead. The fit will be snug. Secure this row of beads to the center of the wooden bead. Have the thread coming out of a black bead with a gold bead to its left.

PATTERN FOR CHEVRON BEAD:

Center row (rows 1 & 2 counting on the diagonal): 2 black, 2 gold.

Row 3: 1 gold, 1 black.

Row 4: 1 black, 1 gold.

Row 5: 1 gold, 1 black.

Row 6: Decrease, 1 gold, 1 black, 1 gold.

Row 7: 1 black, 1 gold, 2 black, 1 gold, 2 black, 1 gold, 2 black, 1 gold, 1 black.

Row 8: 1 gold, 1 black, 2 gold, 1 black, 2 gold, 1 black, 2 gold, 1 black, 1 gold.

Row 9: 1 black, 1 gold, 2 black, 1 gold, 2 black, 1 gold, 2 black, 1 gold, 1 black.

Row 10: 1 gold, decrease, 2 gold, decrease, 2 gold, decrease, 2 gold, decrease, 1 gold.

Row 11: all black.

Row 12: all gold.

8. Sew through this last row of beads again to secure. Weave back to the center row, turn the wooden bead upside down so that the black and gold beads are on top. The needle should exit a gold bead heading to the left. The second half of the pattern is as follows.

Row 3a: 1 gold, 1 black.

Row 4a: 1 gold, 1 black.

Row 5a: 1 gold, 1 black.

Row 6a: decrease, 1 black, 1 gold, 1 black.

Row 7a: 1 black, 2 gold.

Row 8a: 2 black, 1 gold.

Row 9a: 1 gold, 1 black, 2 gold, 1 black, 2 gold, 1 black, 2 gold, 1 black, 1 gold.

Row 10a: 1 black, decrease, 2 black, decrease, 2 black, decrease, 2 black, decrease, 1 black.

Row 11a: all gold.

Row 12a: all black.

9. Sew through this last row of beads again to secure and tie off the thread.

NOTE: Each bead that you make may vary and therefore the exact count may vary by a bead or two, but the overall effect should still be the same.

10. Make 20 spacer beads. Directions for one follow.

SPACER BEADS

These even-count tubular peyote beads have a ruffled edge. On this necklace, they separate (or space) the large beaded beads.

Rows 1 & 2: String on 10 black beads and tie into a circle.

Rows 3 & 4: Black.

Rows 5: Gold.

Rows 6, 7, 8 & 9: Black.

Row 10: Put 3 gold beads in each space to form a simple ruffle. Weave back to the other end and do the same. Weave into the piece and tie off.

11. When all the beads and spacer beads are finished, string them onto the black cording. Adjust the length of the necklace to your liking and knot. Hide the knot in a bead.

12. Now a peyote stitch beaded tube is done around the cording. String 10 black beads on a thread and tie them around the cord. Work tubular peyote to cover the cord, alternating four rows of black with one row of gold. Put simple ruffles on the ends.

13. The surface embellishment is done on the peyote tube with the 15° gold seed beads. Starting at one end, add a thread and exit a gold bead. Pick up five gold 15° beads and spiral down to the next row of gold beads in the tube. Pass the needle through a gold bead. Continue in this downward spiral, adding five surface beads between each attachment to the tube. When you have finished, repeat the process, starting two gold beads to the left of where you began.

Brick Stitch

Also widely known as Comanche stitch, brick stitch takes its name from the horizontal pattern resembling a brick wall. It looks like peyote stitch turned on its side, but the technique is totally different. Each bead is attached to the thread that connects the beads in the previous row. The stitch is a bit more suited to irregular shapes than peyote.

Many beadwork vessels and baskets are made with the circular and tubular forms of this stitch; two are offered as projects in this chapter.

KATHY SEELY Connections, *basket,*
2 in. x 3 in. (5 x 7.5 cm),
brick stitch, 11° seed beads.

Flat Brick Stitch

Flat brick stitch begins with a bead ladder, from which subsequent rows hang.

Figure 1. To make the ladder, pick up two beads and loop back through them twice. To attach the next bead and all others, pick up a bead and loop through the previous bead twice. Do this for the length desired.

NOTE: For clarity in the drawings, I have shown only one loop of thread through previous beads, and the ladder can be done that way. Two loops, however, give you more stability while beading.

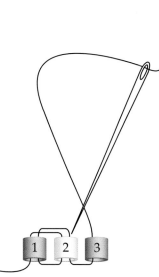

Figure 1.

Figure 2.

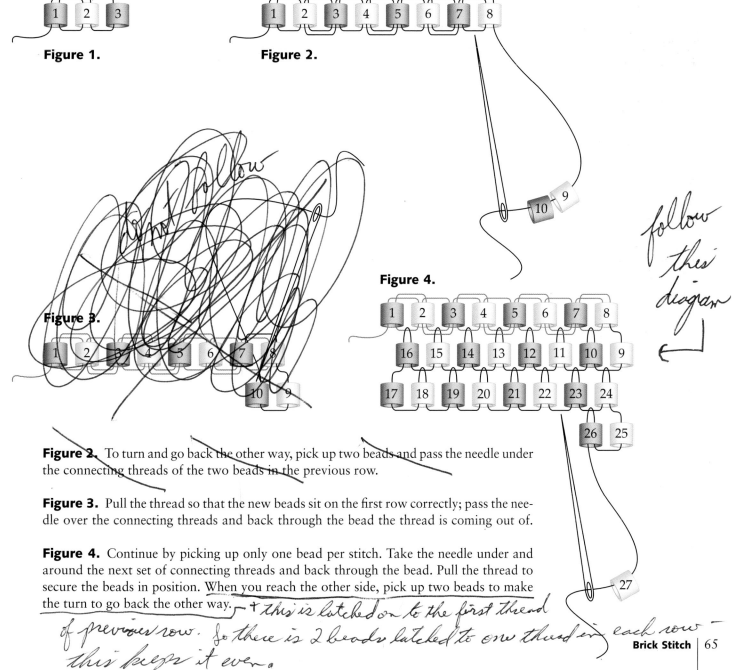

first follow

follow this diagram ←

Figure 4.

Figure 2. To turn and go back the other way, pick up two beads and pass the needle under the connecting threads of the two beads in the previous row.

Figure 3. Pull the thread so that the new beads sit on the first row correctly; pass the needle over the connecting threads and back through the bead the thread is coming out of.

Figure 4. Continue by picking up only one bead per stitch. Take the needle under and around the next set of connecting threads and back through the bead. Pull the thread to secure the beads in position. When you reach the other side, pick up two beads to make the turn to go back the other way. — *this is latched on to the first thread of previous row. So there is 2 beads latched to one thread in each row — this keeps it even.*

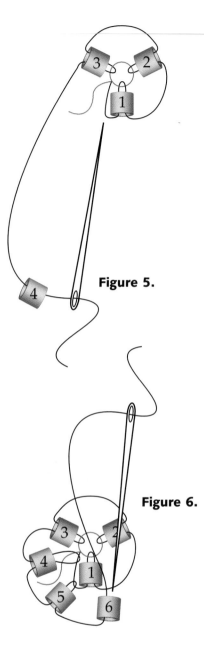

Figure 5.

Figure 6.

Circular Brick Stitch

Circular brick stitch can spiral around its center or form concentric circles. These diagrams show both techniques. The number of beads used on the initial ring is just a suggestion, and the number of beads added to the next row will be determined by the size of the beads that are being used. Increase the number of beads as often as necessary to achieve a solid surface.

CIRCULAR SPIRAL

Figure 5. Make a slip knot, with the tail end of the thread as the piece that slides. Pick up one bead. Pass the needle through the loop of the slip knot and back into the same bead. Pull the thread to draw the bead up close to the slip knot loop. Add two more beads to the ring of thread in the same manner. Then carefully pull the sliding tail of the slip knot to close up the circle.

Figure 6. The next bead that is put on attaches to the thread that is on the outside of the first bead. Pick up a bead, then pass the needle under and over the thread and back into the same bead. Add another bead to that same thread if needed. Continue working around, adding beads to the threads that connect the previous row of beads. The beads will spiral around the center.

 JOANN BAUMANN Beads and Waves, *basket, 3¾ in. x 3¾ in. x 3¾ in. (9.5 cm x 9.5 cm x 9.5 cm), brick stitch, peyote ruffles, and fringes, assorted glass seed beads and Baumann's lampworked beads.*

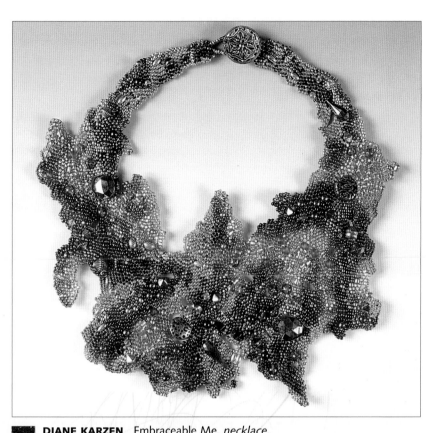

DIANE KARZEN Embraceable Me, *necklace,*
8½ in. x 8½ in. (21 cm), brick stitch, 11° seed
beads and other assorted beads.

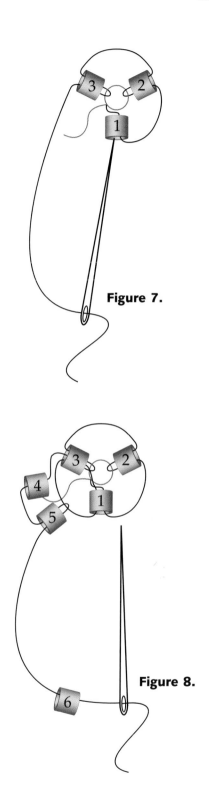

Figure 7.

Figure 8.

CIRCULAR CONCENTRIC

Figure 7. Start with the slip knot again. Instead of picking up one bead, as in Figure 1, pick up two beads. Pass the needle through the slip knot loop and back into bead #2. The first bead just sits next to the second bead for now. Add the third bead to the thread loop, tighten the slip knot, and pass the needle up through bead #1 and down through bead #3.

Figure 8. Pick up two beads, #4 and #5, to begin the next row and every row thereafter. Attach the last bead of each row to the first bead of that row.

If you are working in the spiral method and want to change to the concentric, at any point in the row pick up two beads instead of one. When you reach that first bead again, pass the needle up through it and back down the last one added. Pick up two beads and continue in the concentric method.

To move from concentric to spiral, at the beginning of a row pick up one bead; when you reach it again, use the thread on the outside of the bead to attach the next bead. A spiral pattern will occur.

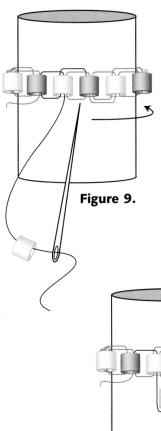

Figure 9.

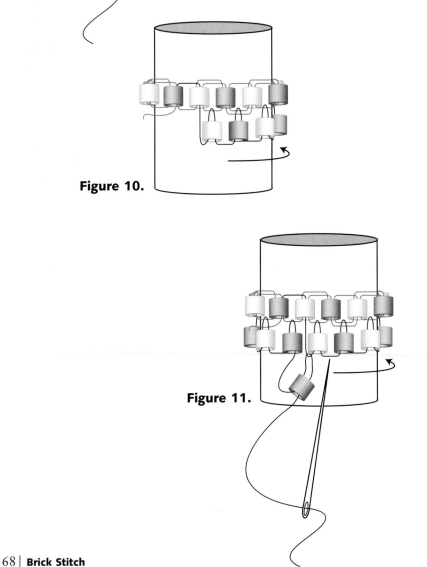

Figure 10.

Figure 11.

Tubular Brick Stitch

Like circular brick stitch, tubular brick can be made to spiral or form concentric circles.

TUBULAR SPIRAL

Figure 9. Make a bead ladder the desired length, following the instructions for flat brick stitch (see Figures 1 and 2). Join the two ends by looping the thread through the end beads. Pick up a bead and, moving to the right, loop around the connecting threads in the bead ladder.

Figure 10. Continue the row in the same way.

Figure 11. Upon reaching the end of the row, attach the next bead to the thread that is on the outside of the first bead of that row.

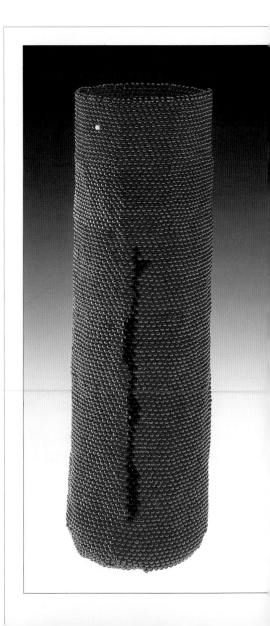

TUBULAR CONCENTRIC

Figure 12. After connecting the ends of the bead ladder, pick up two beads.

Figure 13. Attach the second bead to the first set of threads in the bead ladder. Continue around, adding one bead at a time.

Figure 14. At the end of the row, pass the needle through the first bead of the row and back down through the last bead of the row. Pick up two beads to begin the next and all following rows.

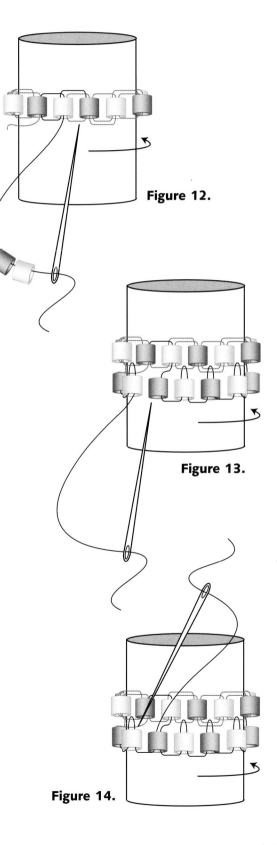

Figure 12.

Figure 13.

Figure 14.

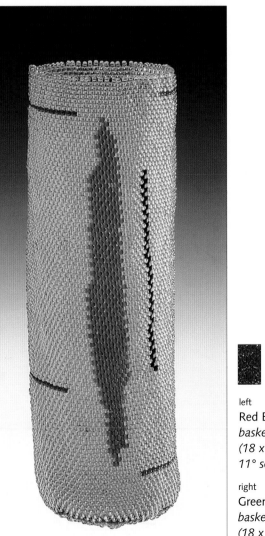

JEANNINE ANDERSON GORESKI

left
Red Band,
basket, 7 in. x 2 in. (18 x 5 cm), brick stitch, 11° seed beads.

right
Green River Memories,
basket, 7 in. x 2 in. (18 x 5 cm), brick stitch, 11° seed beads.

Increasing and Decreasing

In brick stitch, these techniques are fairly straightforward.

INCREASING ON THE OUTSIDE EDGES

This technique is for flat brick stitch.

Figure 15. To increase on an outside edge, start adding beads to the row that you are on, looping them together as you would to start a new flat piece.

Figure 16. When the desired length is reached, pick up two beads, turn, and go back the other way.

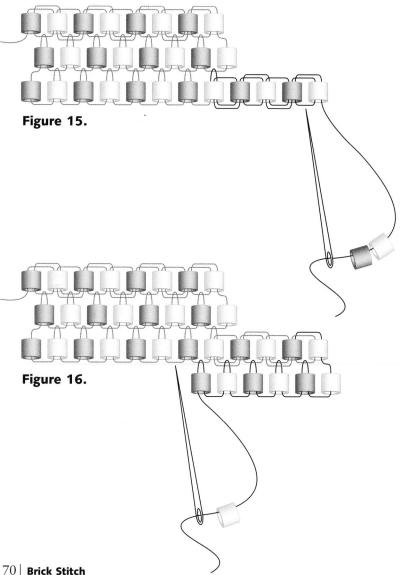

Figure 15.

Figure 16.

FRAN STONE   Egyptian Collar, *11 in. x 8 in.*
(28 x 20.5 cm), brick stitch, 8° hex beads,
11° seed beads, and Czech fire-polished beads.

INCREASING WITHIN A PIECE

This technique can be used on flat or tubular brick stitch.

Figure 17. To increase within a piece, add two beads to the same connecting thread. This is done by adding one bead in the usual manner, then adding another to the same thread.

Figure 18. Upon reaching the increased beads on the next row, treat each connecting thread as one.

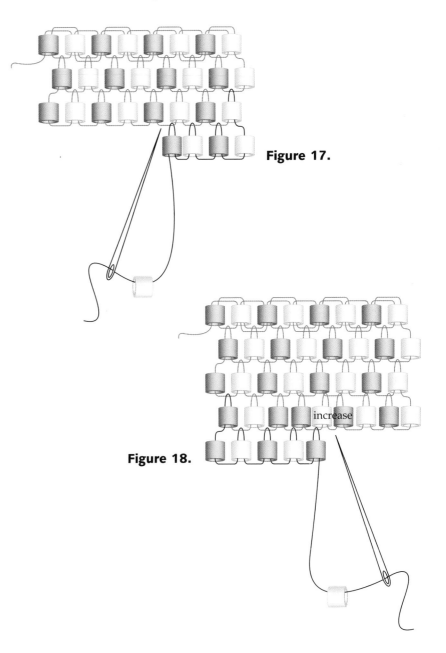

Figure 17.

Figure 18.

increase

Figure 19.

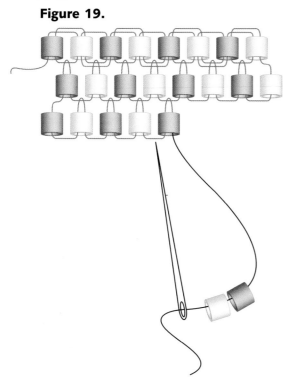

DECREASING ON THE OUTSIDE EDGE

This technique is for the flat stitch.

Figure 19. One way to decrease a piece of flat brick stitch is simply to stop adding beads before you reach the end of the row.

Figure 20. For a gradual, stepped decrease, the needle will have to be repositioned before adding beads to the next row. This is done by finishing a row and weaving up through the neighboring bead, into and out of the pervious row, and back down. Now two beads can be picked up and the row continued.

Figure 21. This illustration shows the turn on the other side.

Figure 20.

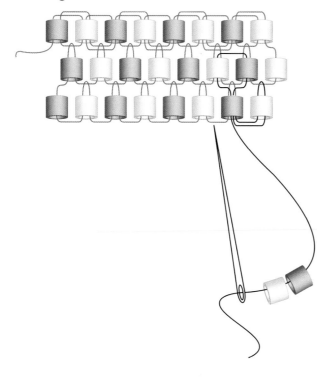

Figure 21.

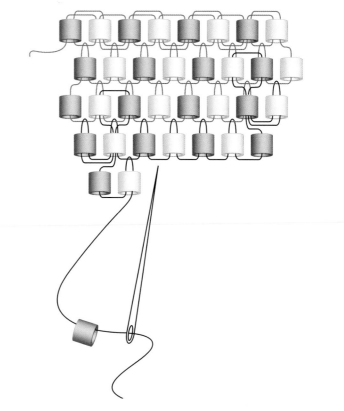

GINI WILLIAMS   Miranda Basket, *6 in. x 12 in. x 8 in. (15 x 30.5 x 20.5 cm), four-drop brick stitch over a basket with free-form peyote stitch embellishments, lined with machine-embroidered fabric, 11° seed beads.*

DECREASING WITHIN A PIECE

This method of decreasing can be used on flat or tubular brick stitch.

Figure 22. To decrease within a piece, flat or tubular, skip a connecting thread, pull the thread tight to close up the space, and continue stitching.

Figure 23. The next row is regular brick stitch all the way across.

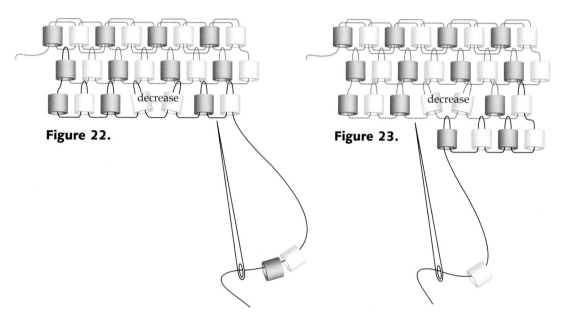

Figure 22.

Figure 23.

TWO-DROP (AND MORE)

Working brick stitch in two-drop, three-drop, or even more makes a project go faster, which is especially useful when you're covering a large object. Instead of picking up one bead per stitch, pick up several and use them as one.

Figure 24. In this illustration, the first row is single brick stitch and the second row is two-drop. The variations seem endless.

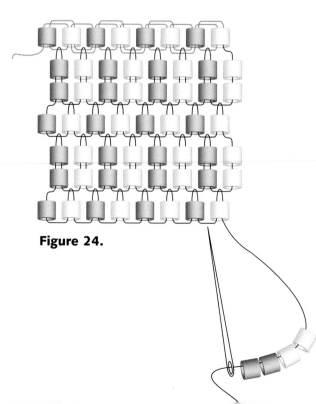

Figure 24.

Attaching Fringe to Brick Stitch

Figure 25. To add fringe to the working edge of brick stitch, come out of a bead and pick up all the beads needed for a piece of fringe. By-passing the last bead, go back up through all the fringe beads and the base bead. Weave over to the next bead and repeat.

If fringe needs to be added to the non-working edge, follow the directions for adding fringe to peyote stitch.

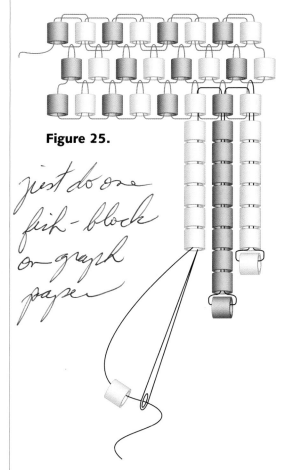

Figure 25.

just do one fish-block on graph paper

ELLA JOHNSON-BENTLEY Gone Fishin, *amulet purse, 4 in. x 2 in. (10 x 5 cm); bugle ladder, brick stitch, and branched fringe; 11° seed beads and other assorted beads.*

project

Ear Rings of Saturn

DESIGNER: **Carol Wilcox Wells**

When confirmed beaders shop for a new outfit, they're always thinking about what beadwork they have that will go with it. If you're caught short and have to make something fast, try these simple earrings. They take only a couple of hours, and they don't require many beads.

MATERIALS

- Beads
  Size 11° cylinder seed beads
    Dark red silver-lined:
      approx. 90 beads
    Gold iris, 22 kt:
      approx. 111 beads
  Size 15° glass seed beads
    Dark red silver-lined:
      approx. 260 beads
  Trim Beads
    2 mm gold-filled beads: 24
    3 mm gold-filled beads: 4
    3.5 x 8 mm gold-filled teardrops: 12

- Beading thread, dark red
- Beading needles, size 12
- Pair of French ear wires, gold
- 2-inch (5 cm) head pin, gold: 2
- Round-nose pliers
- Chain-nose pliers
- Flush cutters

TECHNIQUES USED

✓ Brick stitch, flat

FINISHED SIZE

3 inches x ¼ inch (7.5 x .5 cm)

INSTRUCTIONS

1. Thread the needle with about 4 feet (1.2 m) of thread. Leaving an 8-inch (20.5 cm) tail, work flat brick stitch, following the graph in Figure 1. Don't tie off either thread yet.

2. Add a needle to the tail thread, roll the brick stitch piece up until the opposite sides come together and interlock. Weave the sides together with the tail thread. Tie this thread off within the piece.

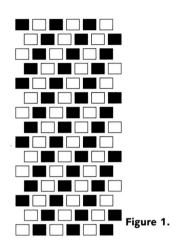

Figure 1.

3. Put a 3 mm gold bead onto a head pin. Slide the bead tube on next, keeping the working thread toward the bottom of the head pin. Now add another 3 mm gold bead. Using chain-nose pliers placed close to the last gold bead, bend the head pin to a 90° angle. Now use the round-nose pliers to form a closed loop, then coil the excess wire around the head pin until it touches the top of the gold bead. Cut the leftover wire close to the base and bend inward to eliminate a rough edge.

4. Six fringes hang from the six beads on the lower edge of the brick stitch tube. Each fringe is consecutively longer than the last one. Using the working thread, make the first fringe.

Fringe #1. Coming out of a gold bead, add four sets of one gold plus one 15° red. Then add one 2 mm gold bead, one gold teardrop, and one 2 mm gold bead.

Fringe #2. Coming out of a red bead, add 12 15° red, one 2 mm gold bead, one gold teardrop, and one 2 mm gold bead.

Fringe #3. Coming out of a gold bead, add seven sets of one gold plus one 15° red. Then add one 2 mm gold bead, one gold teardrop, and one 2 mm gold bead.

Fringe #4. Coming out of a gold bead, add 20 15° red, then one 2 mm gold bead, one gold teardrop, and one 2 mm gold bead.

Fringe #5. Coming out of a gold bead, add 10 sets of one gold plus one 15° red, then one 2 mm gold bead, one gold teardrop, and one 2 mm gold bead.

Fringe #6. Coming out of a gold bead, add 26 15° red, one 2 mm gold bead, one gold teardrop, and one 2 mm gold bead.

NOTE: To make the pair of earrings mirror images of each other—so that the shortest fringe is on the inside of both earrings, for example—reverse the order of the fringes for the second earring.

5. After the last fringe is completed, the needle and thread should be exiting a red base bead. String on 17 15° red beads, loop the thread around the tube, and pass the needle through the beads again. A ring of beads will have been formed around the brick stitch tube. Make sure that the ring is tight. Carefully thread the needle up through four rows of beads on the base tube. Make another red ring of beads, thread through four more beads, and make the last saturn ring.

6. Tie off the thread and add an ear wire.

7. Repeat for second earring.

Unfolding

DESIGNER: **Kathy Seely**

This little vessel is a study in form and light. When placed in a sunny window, it glows with energy and transforms the space around it. The combination of transparent and opaque beads contributes to this phenomenon.

MATERIALS

- Beads

    Size 11° seed beads

    Opaque light purple: 20 grams

    Transparent lavender matte iridescent: 10 grams

    Transparent light lavender: 10 grams

    Opaque dark purple: 10 grams

    Opaque matte purple: 10 grams

    Transparent dark amethyst: 10 grams

- 2-inch-diameter (5 cm) plastic foam ball
- Gesso (a canvas preparer available where artists' supplies are sold)
- Beading thread, gray
- Beading needles, size 12
- Skewer or knitting needle
- Straight pins
- Pencil, eraser, and ballpoint pen

TECHNIQUES USED

✓ Brick stitch: flat, circular spiral, and tubular

✓ Increasing and decreasing

FINISHED SIZE

2 x 2¼ x 2¼ inches (5 x 6 x 6 cm)

INSTRUCTIONS

PREPARING THE ARMATURE

1. Flatten the bottom of the foam ball by pressing it hard onto a flat surface; the flat bottom should be about 1 inch (2.5 cm) in diameter. Stick the wooden skewer or knitting needle into the end of the ball opposite the flattened end.

2. Paint the ball with gesso, applying at least two coats and letting each one

dry thoroughly. Check the ball for smoothness; if it's still rough, sand it with fine sandpaper and paint it again.

DRAWING THE DESIGN

3. Using a pencil, transfer the drawing in Figure 1 to the foam ball. There will be 10 points equally spaced around the form. If you make mistakes, erase and redraw. When satisfied, go over the lines with a ballpoint pen.

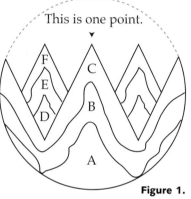

This is one point.

Figure 1.

COLOR CHART:

A - Opaque light purple
B - Transparent lavender matte
C - Transparent light lavender
D - Opaque dark purple
E - Opaque purple matte
F - Transparent dark amethyst

BEADING THE VESSEL

Before starting, remember to keep the tension even and a little on the snug side but not too tight. If the tension is too loose, the vessel will be floppy. If it's too tight, the bowl will have ripples.

4. Following the directions for circular spiral brick stitch, put four beads onto the slip knot. Increasing when necessary, spiral around until the piece is about ¾ inch (2 cm) in diameter.

5. It is now time to attach the beads to the form. Place a pin through the center of the circle of beads and push the pin into the center of the flattened bottom of the foam ball. Place a few more pins around to secure the position of the beads.

6. Continue beading on the form until you reach the edges of the flattened bottom. Reposition the beads if they are not properly centered on the bottom of the form.

NOTE: Watch how the beads are lying on the form. If there are ruffles on the edges, you are increasing too much. If the beads want to cup up all around, you are not increasing enough. The beads should lie flat against the form.

7. Weave tubular brick stitch up the sides of the form, following the pattern for the color placement. As the work progresses beyond the widest part of the form begin decreasing slowly and evenly.

8. When you reach the place where the petals of the design begin to separate, bead them individually in flat brick stitch.

REMOVING THE FORM

9. Crush the exposed portion of the foam ball and carefully try to remove it from the beaded vessel. You may have to break it up into chunks and crush it some more until it will come out easily. Be careful not to damage the beadwork.

Clay Bead Vessel
DESIGNER: **NanC Meinhardt**

This vessel was designed to have a primitive appearance, and in fact it looks like a treasure unearthed during an archaeological dig. The beads are rippled clay tubes of varying lengths. Each tube looks as though it were several individual beads. These beads have unfinished edges, which means they can cut thread easily; sand the ends carefully and reinforce the work by passing the thread through each bead more than once.

MATERIALS
The quantities of beads will vary, depending on their size. The following list is only a guideline.

- Beads
  African clay beads ranging from ¹⁄₁₆ inch to ³⁄₈ inch (2 mm to 1 cm): 1058
  African heishi beads (flat disks): 347
  Size 11° cut seed beads, silver: 560
  Size 11° seed beads, ivory: 275
  Size 11° seed beads, matte beige: 40
  Embellishing beads made of glass, wood, bone, silver, and clay: 3 mm, 4 mm, and /or 5 mm: 80

- Twisted beading thread, tan
- Beading needles, size 10

TECHNIQUES USED
✓ Brick stitch, circular spiral and tubular spiral
✓ Increasing and decreasing
✓ Brick stitch peyote edging

FINISHED SIZE
3 x 4 x 4 inches (7.5 x 10 x 10 cm)

INSTRUCTIONS

1. Rows 1 through 4 make up the bottom of the vessel and are done in circular spiral brick stitch. Begin by putting on 8 clay beads about ³⁄₁₆ inch (6 mm) long onto the loop of a slip knot. This is row 1. Work three more rows, increasing as necessary to keep it flat.

2. After the fourth row is complete, pull on the thread and beads to begin shaping the sides of the vessel. For rows 5 through 12, continue spiraling upward, working in tubular spiral brick stitch and increasing each row as necessary to shape the vessel. The length of the beads can vary by row.

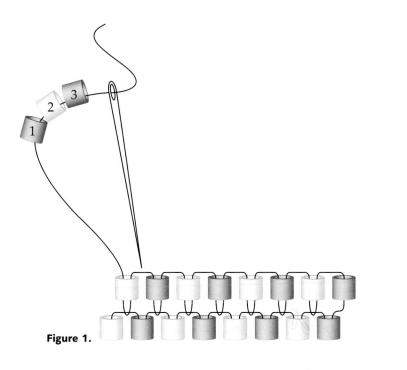

Figure 1.

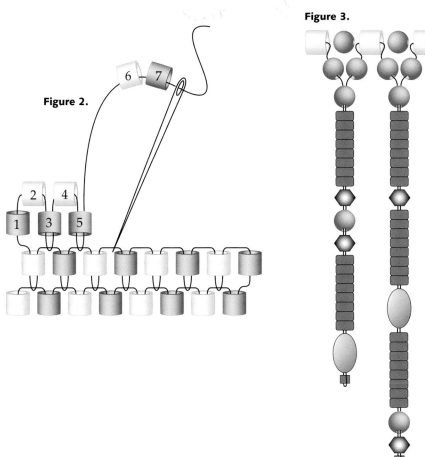

Figure 2.

Figure 3.

3. Switch to the Heishi beads for the row 13, then to 11° cut silver seed beads for row 14, then back to Heishi for row 15. By now, the diameter of the basket should be about 3 inches (7.5 cm) across.

NOTE: The size of beads and number of increases made per row will define the size of your vessel. A primitive look is what you are striving for, not an exact copy.

4. Work rows 16 through 19 with the clay beads. To draw the upper portion of the vessel inward, start a slight decreasing with row 19. For row 20, use beads that are about ¼ inch (.5 cm) long.

5. Work row 21 with the Heishi beads and row 22 with 11° cut silver seed beads.

6. For row 23, make a brick stitch peyote edging, alternating cut silver beads with Heishi beads. See Figures 1 and 2. Then do a row of tubular peyote stitch, alternating beads again. This is the top of your vessel.

7. Now add the surface embellishment. Come out of a clay bead in row 19, add one cut silver bead, and pass the thread back through that same clay bead. Pass the needle through the next clay bead, pick up a silver bead, and attach it. Repeat the above process all the way around the row.

8. Pass the needle through an added silver bead, string on an ivory or beige seed bead, and go through the next silver bead. Continue around the row, filling the spaces with seed beads.

9. Add fringes ¾ inch to 1 inch (2 to 2.5 cm) long, hanging them from the cut silver beads. See Figure 3.

Square Stitch

**SUSAN GEISERT
AND ANN GEISERT,**

Chicago Skyline
Bracelet *and*
Holiday Brights
Bracelet,

*7½ in. x 1 in.
(19 cm x 2.5 cm)
and 7½ in. x ½ in.
(19 cm x 1.5 cm),
square stitch,
11° cylinder
seed beads.*

Square stitch is an off-loom technique that simulates the look of loomwork—without the hassle of tieing off all those warp threads. The beads sit directly above, below, and beside each other, allowing for straight horizontal and vertical lines. The stitch works particularly well with cylinder seed beads.

Square stitch is extremely strong. There are so many threads passing through each bead that there's virtually no chance of it falling apart.

The tubular form of square stitch can be done with or without a form. Because of the way the beads sit, wonderful patterns can be achieved.

Flat Square Stitch

Figure 1. Begin by looping through one bead, positioned about 6 inches (15 cm) from the end of the thread. String on as many beads as needed for the width of the project. To turn, pick up another bead and pass the needle through the bead directly above, then go through the bead that you are putting on. Pick up another bead and repeat the above process. Do this all the way across the piece.

Figure 2. When the row is done, pass the needle through the entire previous row and through the row that has just been finished. This will reinforce and stabilize the work. Do this after the completion of every row.

Figure 3. Note the position you will be in to start the next row after the pass-throughs are completed.

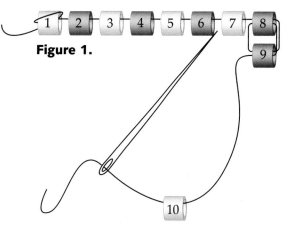

Figure 1.

Figure 2.

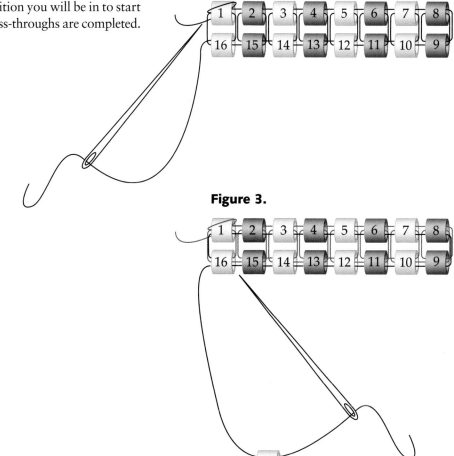

Figure 3.

Tubular Square Stitch

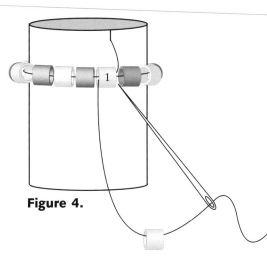

Figure 4.

Figure 4. String on as many beads as needed. Tie them into a ring and slide them onto the form. Pass the needle through a bead (#1) to hide the knot.

Figure 5. Do square stitch around the form in the usual manner.

Figure 6. When the row is finished, pass the needle through all the beads again, exiting the first bead of that row.

The direction of the thread determines the way that you will work around the form. The illustration goes from left to right on row 2 and from right to left on row 3. The first bead of each row sits directly under the first bead of the previous row.

Figure 5.

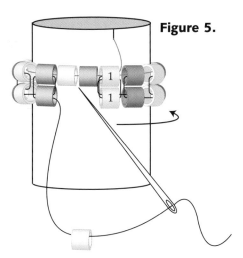

Figure 6.

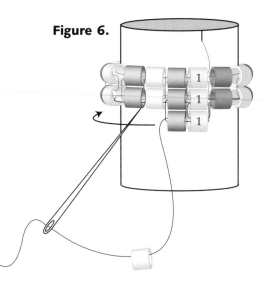

Increasing and Decreasing

INCREASING ON THE OUTSIDE EDGES

Before increasing on an outside edge, first complete the row to its initial length, including passing the thread through the entire row to stabilize it.

Figure 7. Pick up the number of beads you're increasing by plus the first bead of the next row. (In Figure 7, you would pick up three beads.) Using the pass-through thread, loop those last two end beads together and continue down the row.

If you need to increase on the other end, do so before you make the pass-through for this row; this will give you a symmetrical increase. See Figure 7a.

NOTE: You cannot increase just one horizontal row. The increase will affect both the row that has just been finished and the next new row.

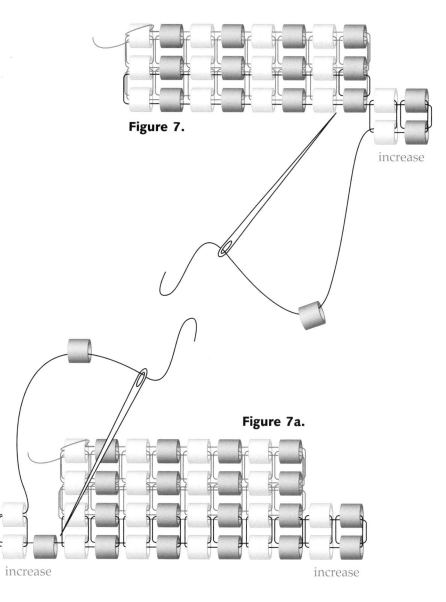

Figure 7.

increase

Figure 7a.

increase

increase

Figure 8.

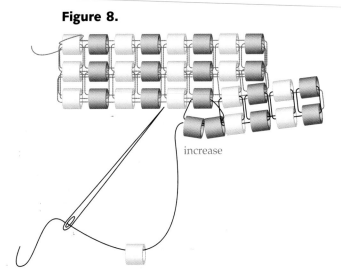

increase

INCREASING WITHIN

Figure 8. When an increase is needed in the middle of a piece, just pick up two beads instead of one for a particular stitch. Upon reaching those beads in the next row, use them individually. You will have increased by one vertical row.

DECREASING ON THE OUTSIDE EDGES

Figure 9. To decrease on an outside edge, exit the bead above where the next row will start.

Figure 10. Do square stitch for the length desired and then pass through the beads that were used in the previous row.

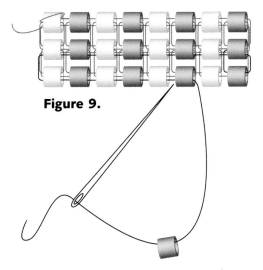

Figure 9.

Figure 10.

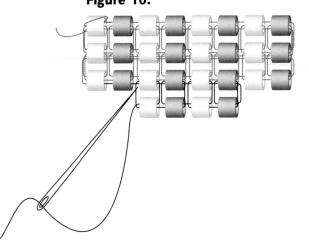

DECREASING WITHIN

This technique works for both flat and tubular square stitch.

Figure 11. To decrease in the middle, skip over a bead, pull the thread snug, and continue square stitching across the row.

When the decrease is reached on the next row, use the two pulled-together beads individually.

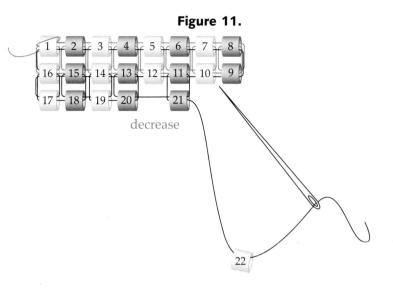

Figure 11.

decrease

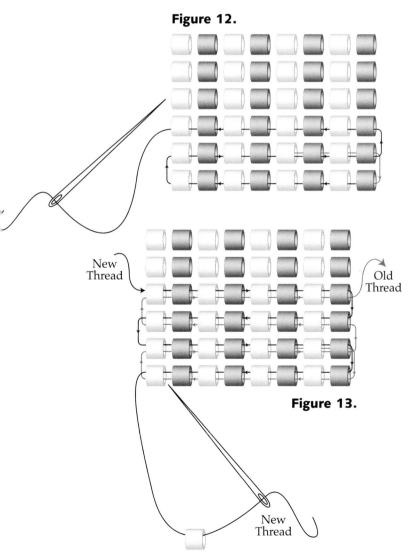

Figure 12.

Figure 13.

New Thread

Old Thread

New Thread

Ending and Adding Thread

In square stitch, there's no need to knot when ending an old thread and adding a new one. There are so many threads in each bead that when another thread is simply woven in, it will hold.

Figure 12. End a thread by weaving back and forth across several rows, then cut the thread as close to the beads as possible.

Figure 13. Add the new thread to the same row but at the opposite end, so the old and new threads are running in the same direction through the beads.

project

Tapestry Bracelet

DESIGNERS:
Susan and Ann Geisert

This simple bracelet is a great way to try out different color combinations to see how they affect each other. The entire bracelet is square stitch, 10 beads wide. Feel free to use completely different colors and to vary the patterns any way you like.

MATERIALS
- Beads
  Size 11° cylinder seed beads
    in 19 colors (very small amounts)

- Beading thread, brown
- Beading needles, size 12
- Gold hook-and-eye clasp

TECHNIQUES USED
✓ Square stitch, flat
✓ Decreasing on outside edges

FINISHED SIZE
7½ inches x ½ inch (19 x 1.5 cm)

INSTRUCTIONS

1. Beginning at Row 1, work square stitch for the length of the bracelet, following the graph if desired.

2. Decrease on the outside edges at both ends after the main part of the bracelet is done.

3. Add the clasp by weaving the hook portion to one end of the bracelet and the eye portion to the other.

Figure 1.

Row #1 →

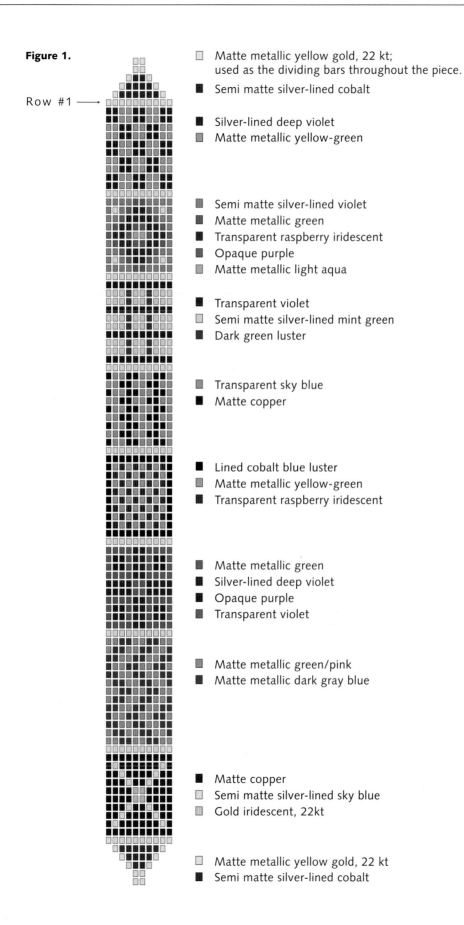

☐ Matte metallic yellow gold, 22 kt;
used as the dividing bars throughout the piece.

■ Semi matte silver-lined cobalt

■ Silver-lined deep violet
▨ Matte metallic yellow-green

▨ Semi matte silver-lined violet
■ Matte metallic green
▦ Transparent raspberry iridescent
■ Opaque purple
▨ Matte metallic light aqua

■ Transparent violet
☐ Semi matte silver-lined mint green
■ Dark green luster

▨ Transparent sky blue
■ Matte copper

■ Lined cobalt blue luster
▨ Matte metallic yellow-green
▦ Transparent raspberry iridescent

■ Matte metallic green
■ Silver-lined deep violet
■ Opaque purple
▨ Transparent violet

▨ Matte metallic green/pink
■ Matte metallic dark gray blue

■ Matte copper
☐ Semi matte silver-lined sky blue
▨ Gold iridescent, 22kt

☐ Matte metallic yellow gold, 22 kt
■ Semi matte silver-lined cobalt

project

Homeward Angel

DESIGNER:
Carol Wilcox Wells

This necklace was designed on the back of a motorcycle, on a round trip to Georgia. The first leg of the trip was miserable—cold, dark, and long. The low point was circling Athens, Georgia, twice by mistake. We finally arrived at our destination, very grumpy indeed. But next day, the trip home was glorious—brilliant sunshine and warm breezes. While husband Bob drove, I graphed Homeward Angel.

MATERIALS

- Beads

  Size 11° cylinder seed beads

  Black opaque: 3 beads; eyes, mouth

  Lined light violet iridescent:
  6 grams; background

  Dark red gold luster:
  9 beads; lips

  Transparent light blue luster:
  8 grams; background

  Copper-lined copper:
  1 gram; hair

  Flesh opal copper-lined:
  6 beads; blush

  Matte copper: 2 grams; wings

  Matte metallic gold, 22kt:
  26 beads; wings

  Matte dark cream:
  5 grams; skin

  Matte light rose:
  1 gram; face shadows

  Gold iris iridescent 22k:
  4 grams; wings and stars

  Silver-lined smoked topaz:
  1 gram; hair and eyebrows

  Trim beads

  2 mm gold beads: 12

  4 mm round pearls: 6

  4 mm blue fire-polished beads: 6

- Beading thread, blue
- Beading needles, size 12
- 4-inch (10 cm) head pin
- 2 gold jump rings
- 20-inch (51 cm) gold chain with open-style links
- Wire cutters

TECHNIQUES USED

✓ Square stitch: flat

✓ Square stitch: increasing and decreasing on outside edges

✓ Surface embellishment

FINISHED SIZE

4 inches x 3½ inches (10 x 9 cm)

INSTRUCTIONS

1. Following the graph in Figure 1, begin square stitching from the top of the large middle section, working your way across and back. Leave an extra-long thread for the tail, as it will be used to attach the panel to the head pin. Increase and decrease as needed to achieve the pattern.

The angel's nose is three-dimensional; a second layer of beads sits on top of the flat foundation. After you've completed the large middle section, take the needle back through the piece until you're in position. Then square stitch the nose beads to the piece.

2. Stitch the two side panels. Add a pearl, a 2 mm gold bead, the 4 mm fire-polished bead, and another 2 mm gold bead as fringe to the ends of both these panels.

3. There are four twisted fringes. For each one, string the following beads onto a 20-inch (51 cm) thread. Do not knot the end of the thread.

    2 mm gold bead: 1
    4 mm blue fire-polished: 1
    2 mm gold bead: 1
    4 mm pearl: 1

    Cylinder seed beads, size 11°:
        light violet: 20
        light blue: 2
        light violet: 2
        light blue: 2
        light violet: 14
        light blue: 2
        light violet: 2
        light blue: 2
        light violet: 2
        light blue: 2
        light violet: 20

Add a needle to the other end of the thread; you now have needles at both ends. Arrange the beads so that they are in the middle of the thread, and secure the thread with tape to the desk top right above the first gold bead.

Now start twisting the untaped needle and thread end. Twist it until the thread really starts to twist upon itself and you can no longer pull it straight. Then carefully pass the needle through the pearl, gold bead, fire-polished bead and gold bead, making sure that all the thread has made it through. The seed beads should now twist upon themselves with a little help from you.

Finish by weaving each thread end up through the fire-polished bead, bypassing the first gold bead and up into the seed beads to tie off.

Make three more twisted fringes.

4. With wire cutters, cut the head off the head pin as close to the end as possible. Measure ¼ inch (.5 cm) from each end and form a closed loop at each end.

Cut the chain in the middle. Using a jump ring, attach the head pin bar to the chain at one end.

5. Slide one of the twisted fringes onto the bar. Then lay one of the small side panels over the bar and roll the beads around it. Put a needle on the tail thread, unlooping it first, and use it to sew a casing around the head pin. See Figure 2.

Slide on another twisted fringe and attach the main panel to the bar. Add another fringe, the last side panel, and the last side fringe.

Using a jump ring, attach the chain to the bar.

Figure 2.

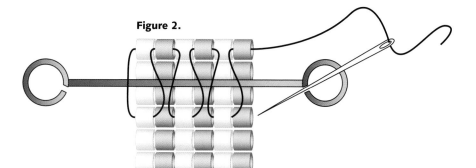

NOTE: *This illustration shows technique, not actual width.*

- ■ Black opaque
- ■ Lined light violet iridescent
- ■ Dark red gold luster
- ☐ Transparent light blue luster
- ▨ Copper-lined copper
- ▨ Flesh opal copper-lined
- ■ Matte copper
- ▨ Matte metallic gold, 22kt
- ☐ Matte dark cream
- ▨ Matte light rose
- ▨ Gold iris 22k
- ■ Silver-lined smoked topaz

Right-Angle Weave

Right-angle weave has a fluidity that other off-loom stitches cannot seem to match. The way the beads sit with each other and the way they are held together produce this effect. Each bead is at a right angle to its neighboring bead, and the thread is also passing at right angles as it joins the sets of beads together.

Right-angle weave can be done with one bead per side, as shown in the illustrations, or with multiple beads on each side. If you look carefully at the detail of the 17th-century English basket on page 6, you will see that the leaves at the top of the photo are done with a 2-1-2-1 configuration. The combinations seem endless and full of promise for exciting beadwork.

The tubular form of this stitch can be used to cover objects, to form the body of a very supple purse, and to make baskets.

JANE ALLEY

Sterling Opera Purse,

*6 in. x 5½ in. x ¼ in.
(15 cm x 14 cm x .5 cm),
right-angle weave, sterling silver
beads lined with Japanese
kimono silk.*

Flat Right-Angle Weave

Figure 1. Pick up four beads and tie them into a ring. Pass the needle through beads #1 and #2. String on three more and pass the needle through #2, #5, and #6. Continue in this manner until the desired width is reached.

Figure 2. To turn and go in the opposite direction, exit bead #11, pick up three beads, and go back into #11.

Figure 3. Pass the needle through beads #14, #15, and #16, then through bead #10. Pick up #17 and #18, and go through #16, #10, and #17.

Work your way across, always keeping the thread and the beads at right angles. Never let a thread cross straight through an intersection. Notice that the stitches go from a clockwise direction to a counter-clockwise direction as you work along a row.

Figure 1.

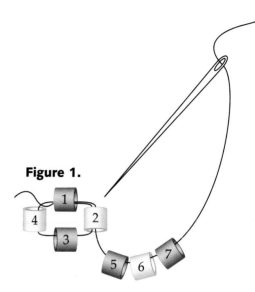

Figure 2.

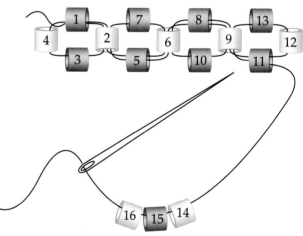

Figure 3.

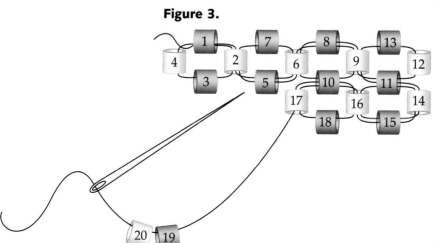

Tubular Right-Angle Weave

Figure 4. Pick up four beads and tie into a ring. Weave through one and start flat right-angle weave. Make the initial strip the length of the circumference of the object that you will be working on.

Figure 5. Join the two ends together by picking up a bead, going through the connector bead on the opposite side, picking up another bead, and going back down through the original connector.

Depending on the number of stitches and on whether the thread is moving in a clockwise or counter-clockwise direction, the ends can be joined exactly as shown or exactly opposite.

Figure 6. To begin the next row, weave down to a horizontal bead and continue with right-angle weave.

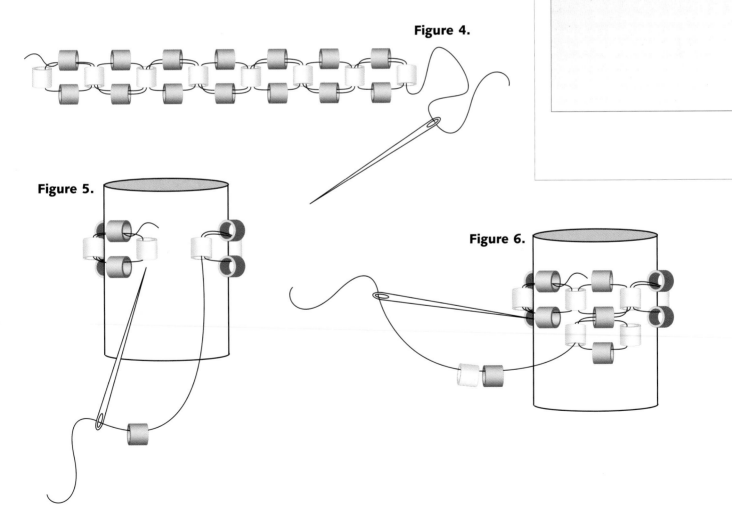

Figure 4.

Figure 5.

Figure 6.

NANC MEINHARDT   Beaded Bead Necklace, *20 in. x 2 in. x 1 in.*
(51 cm x 5 cm x 2.5 cm), right-angle weave, brick stitch, peyote stitch,
11° and 15° seed beads and other assorted beads.

Increasing and Decreasing

INCREASING ON THE OUTSIDE EDGES

Figure 7. In increasing on an outside edge, sets of beads
are added either at the beginning of a row, or at the
end of a row, or both, as shown here. Following the
diagram, pick up beads #14, #15, #16, and #17. Go
back into #14 to make the increase loop, and then
continue across.

When you exit bead #24, pick up the increase beads
#26, #27, and #28, then continue back the other way.

You can increase a piece by any width by adding more
loops of beads at either side.

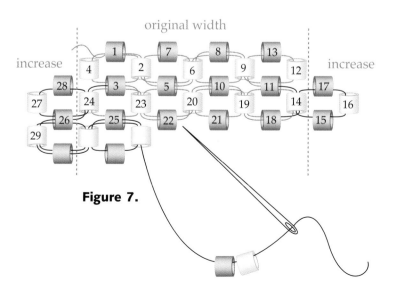

Figure 7.

JOANN BAUMANN Jangles, *basket, 4 in. x 5¼ in. x 5¼ in.*
(10 cm x 13.5 cm x 13.5 cm), right-angle weave using telephone
wire, Baumann's lampworked beads and 6° seed beads.

SUSAN LUTZ KENYON
Enchanted Entity Necklace and Pin, *4 in. x 3 in. (10 cm x 7.5 cm).*
*The bodies are fabric, machine-sewn and stuffed. Beadwork on
the necklace is right-angle weave with fringe for the tunic, and peyote
stitch for the strap. The beadwork on the pin is brick stitch.*

INCREASING WITHIN

Figure 8. To increase within a piece, just add an extra bead to a stitch.

Figure 9. When you reach that stitch on the next row, use the two extra beads as separate connecting beads. There are now five stitches per row instead of four.

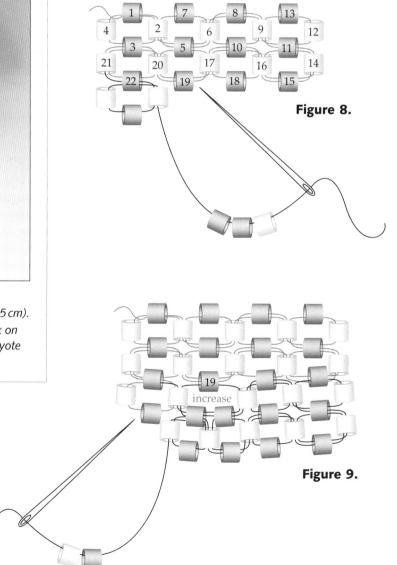

Figure 8.

Figure 9.

DECREASING ON THE OUTSIDE EDGES

Figure 10. To decrease on the outside edges, weave through the beads, keeping at right angles, until you reach the place where you want to begin again.

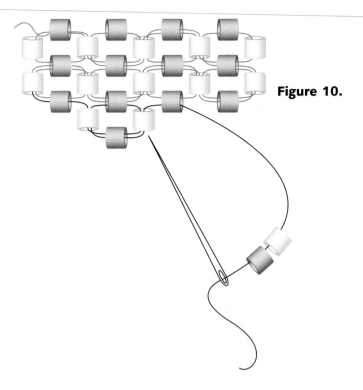

Figure 10.

DECREASING WITHIN

Figure 11. To decrease within a piece, flat or tubular, the needle must pass through two horizontal beads.

Figure 12. As the stitch is completed, pull the thread tight so the beads are pulled together. Continue with right-angle weave.

Figure 11.

decrease

Figure 12.

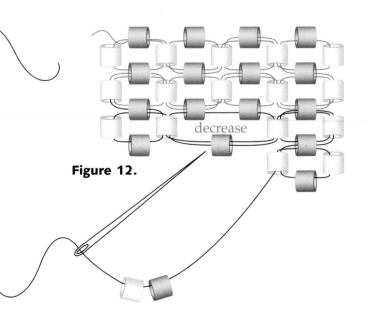

project

Plumed Iris Amulet Purse

DESIGNER: **Julie Goetsch**

Plumed Iris is made with a flat right-angle weave. The spaces are then filled in with larger beads sewn on a diagonal across the open squares.

Figure 1: *Purse Foundation*

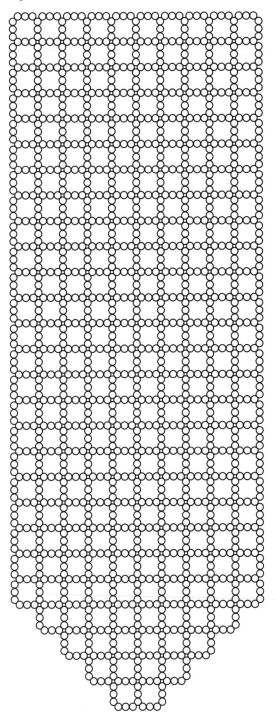

MATERIALS

- Beads (all a blue iris color)
  Size 11° seed beads: 50 grams
  Size 6° seed beads: approx. 350
  3 mm bugles: 22
  12 mm bugles: 22
  4 mm round beads: 22
  Accent beads (twisted
    ovals): 22
  Feather-shaped beads with
    holes through top: 22
  Button, ½ inch (1.5 cm) in
    diameter
- Beading thread, blue
- Beading needles, size 12

TECHNIQUES USED

✓ Right-angle weave, flat
✓ Decreasing on outside edges
✓ Fringe

FINISHED SIZE

5 inches x 2½ inches x ¼ inch
  (12.5 x 6.5 x .5 cm)

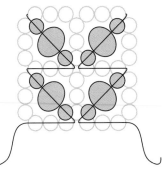

Figure 2:
An enlarged center section of the purse, showing the angle of the surface embellishment beads and how they are sewn on. Work up one vertical row and then down the next.

INSTRUCTIONS

1. Work the foundation of the purse as shown in Figure 1. There are three 11° seed beads on each side of the units, and there are 10 units across, decreasing as shown at the bottom of the diagram.

2. After you have completed the foundation, fill the squares formed by the right-angle weave. See Figure 2. Take the needle through the three beads on one side of a right-angle square. Then string on one 11° seed bead, one 6° seed bead, and one 11° seed bead; take the needle diagonally across the square and go through the three beads on the other side. String on three more beads and continue.

Slant the interior elements toward each other at the center of the pattern so that they are going in one direction in one half of the foundation and in the other direction in the other half of the foundation. See Figure 3.

NOTE: Following Figure 3, omit the above in the shaded areas of this diagram.

3. Fold the foundation piece so that the vacant squares in the center form the bottom of the purse.

4. Join the sides by adding three seed beads at each square, using right-angle weave. Fill each square with the same three-bead elements as before.

5. Continue right-angle weave up from the side to form the strap. After the desired length is reached, attach to the other side. Now fill the squares along the strap.

Figure 3.

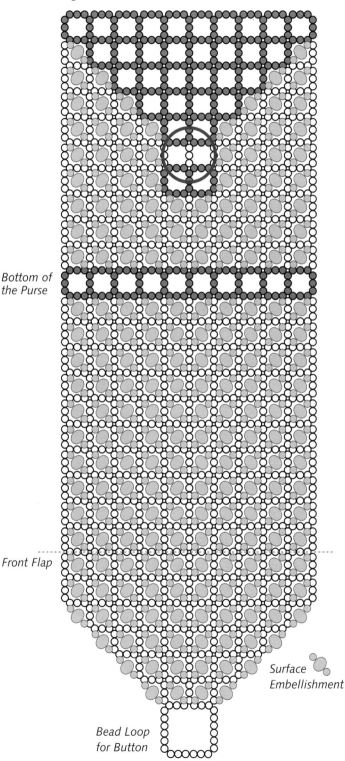

*Bottom of
the Purse*

Front Flap

*Surface
Embellishment*

*Bead Loop
for Button*

6. Form a beaded loop at the bottom of the flap to go around the button for the closure.

7. Attach the button in the position shown by the circle on Figure 3.

8. Make the fringes at the bottom of the purse. The fringes in the front will be slightly shorter than those in the back. There are 11 in the front and 11 in the back. The following is the sequence of beads used:

FRONT

  3 11° seed beads
  1 3 mm bugle bead
  3 11° seed beads
  1 4 mm round bead
  1 12 mm bugle bead
  1 6° seed bead
  3 11° seed beads
  1 twisted oval bead
  4 11° seed beads
  1 feather bead
  4 11° seed beads
Go back into the oval bead and add:
  3 11° seed beads
Pass the needle back up all the beads

BACK

  5 11° seed beads
  1 3 mm bugle bead
  3 11° seed beads
  1 4 mm round bead
  1 12 mm bugle bead
  1 6° seed bead
  3 11° seed beads
  1 twisted oval bead
  4 11° seed beads
  1 feather bead
  4 11° seed beads
Go back into the oval bead and add:
  3 11° seed beads
Pass the needle back up all the beads.

African Helix

Netting

Chevron Chain

While these stitches are not as versatile as peyote, brick, square stitch, and right-angle weave, all three can add interest and texture to your work. They can also be used in nontraditional ways and in combination with other stitches.

 MARLA GASSNER

Turquoise Treasure, *necklace, 17 in. x 3½ in. x ½ in. (43 cm x 9 cm x 1.5 cm), African helix, 11° seed beads, antique glass flower buttons and turquoise.*

Coral Adorned, *necklace, 15½ in. x 3½ in. x ½ in. (39.5 cm x 9 cm x 1.5 cm), African helix, 11° seed beads, antique Chinese carnelian buttons, coral and vintage pressed glass flowers.*

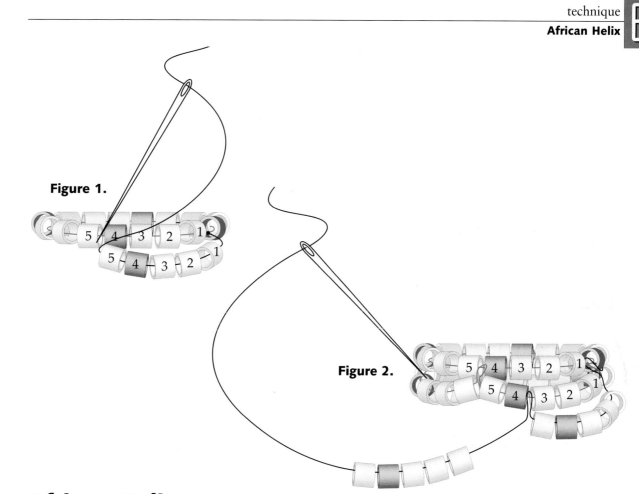

Figure 1.

Figure 2.

African Helix

The African helix makes a very flexible tubular chain. The size of the beads and the number of beads in the initial ring will determine the diameter of the helix.

Figure 1. String on four sets of four beads, with every fourth bead a different color. Tie into a tight ring.

NOTE: I have found it easier to start the helix if the initial ring is put onto a support of some kind—for example, a pencil, dowel, or knitting needle.

Pick up five beads (three light, one dark, one light), and pass the needle down into the ring, looping the working thread around the ring thread between beads #4 and #5.

Continue around the ring, picking up five beads and passing the needle down between the next sets of four. Keep the thread very tight as you are working.

NOTE: Do not pass the needle through any beads. The action of looping the thread around the thread of the previous row is what holds the helix together.

Figure 2. For the third and subsequent rows, pick up five beads and pass the needle down through the previous row of looped beads, positioning the thread between the third and fourth beads. Continue spiraling around until the desired length is reached.

NOTE: To achieve a solid-colored spine, string on three base-colored beads followed by two of the spine color. For a dotted spine, string three base beads followed by one spine and one more base color.

I have tried the helix with tiny bugles as the spine (three 11° seed beads and one 3 mm bugle) and with the bugles replacing the first two seed beads. The effects are interesting, although the bugle spine is somewhat rough against the skin.

Netting

This open-weave stitch is aptly named. It resembles a very elegant fish net.

VERTICAL NETTING

This stitch produces a very supple "fabric" that drapes beautifully. It requires advanced planning, since you are working the entire length of the netting with each row you put on. In these illustrations, the netting hangs from a section of peyote stitch.

Figure 3. String on the entire length of beads needed for the first vertical row. Here I have used 20 beads. Beads #1, #5, #9, #13, and #17 are connector beads and are thus shown in a different color.

End the row by passing the needle back into connector bead #17. Now pick up seven beads and take the needle through bead #9.

Figure 4. Pick up seven more beads and go through bead #1. Weave through the peyote base and exit several beads away. Pick up four beads and pass through a connector bead in the previous row.

Figure 5. Working in a downward motion, pick up seven beads, pass by one connector bead, and weave into the next.

NOTE: Each connector bead will have four spokes radiating from it—two from one side and two from the other.

Figure 6. The netting's characteristic diamond pattern takes shape as you weave.

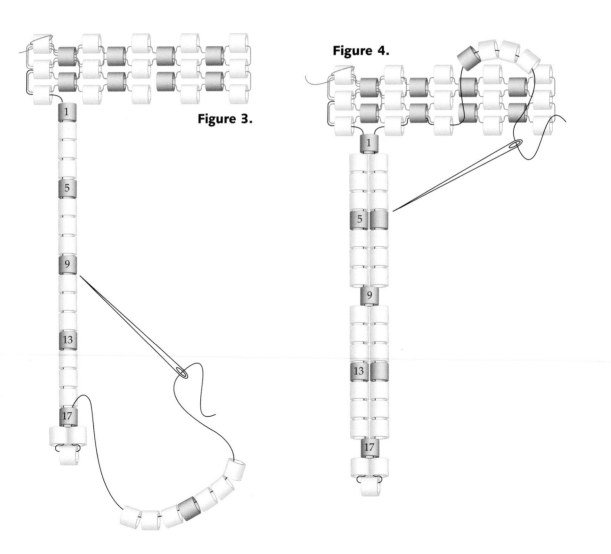

Figure 3.

Figure 4.

NANC MEINHARDT

In Memory of My Father,
*3¾ in. x 2¾ in.
(9.5 cm x 7 cm),
vertical netting connected
to a bead ladder,
11° seed beads and
other assorted beads.*

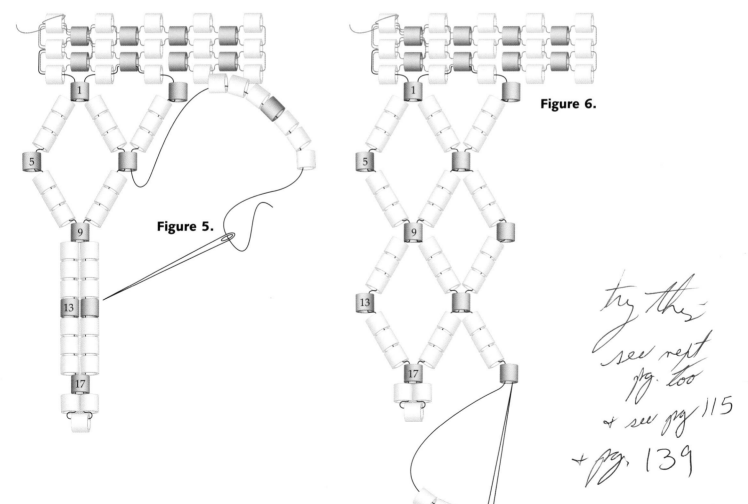

Figure 5.

Figure 6.

HORIZONTAL NETTING

The diamond pattern in horizontal netting is very distinct and holds its shape well. It differs from vertical netting not only in how it is worked but also in the position of some of the beads themselves. Look at connecting beads #12, #19, #8, #37, #30, etc., in Figure 7; note that the thread passes through them horizontally. This does not happen in vertical netting and is what helps maintain its open net structure. Increasing and decreasing can be done on the outside edges.

Horizontal netting requires an odd number of beads in each unit. In Figure 1, the netting has a seven-bead unit and hangs from a piece of peyote.

Figure 7. Exiting the peyote bead on the left, pick up 15 beads. For ease in following the pattern, make beads #4, #8, and #12 a different color. Pass the needle through the third protruding peyote bead, pick up seven beads, and pass the needle through the fifth peyote bead. This pattern of picking up seven and attaching to the base will continue for the width of the piece.

To turn and go back the other way, pick up enough beads for a unit and a half—in this case, 11 beads (seven plus four). Pass the needle through bead #19 and pick up another unit of beads. After passing the needle through bead #12, pick up three beads to complete the first diamond. Attach these to the base and pass the needle through beads #1 through #8. Pick up a unit and attach to bead #37. Continue across and back up to bead #75.

The turns on one side of the netting are a bit more complicated than on the other, and a little weaving is involved to get back into position to begin again.

With the unit of beads that ends with 75 on the thread, pass the needle through beads #47, #46, #45, #44, and #8. Pick up 11 beads and pass the needle through beads #47, #48, #49, #50. By-pass #37 and go into #38, #39, #40, #12, #11, #10, #9, #8, and #76 through #83. You are now ready to begin again.

NOTE: Each connector bead can only have four spokes radiating from it. If there are more or fewer, there is a problem somewhere, and you will need to go back and correct it.

 GINI WILLIAMS
We Didn't Start the Fire,

collar, 10½ in. x 10½ in. (26.5 cm x 26.5 cm), bugle ladders joined with horizontal netting, antique bugle beads and 18°—20° seed beads.

Figure 7.

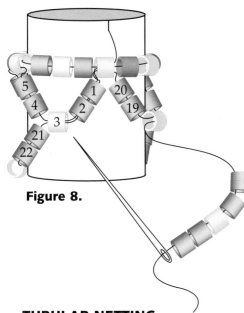

Figure 8.

TUBULAR NETTING

Tubular netting is also worked in a horizontal fashion using an odd number of beads per unit. It is done around an object or form.

Figure 8. The base is a string of beads tied into a ring and slipped over the form. The number of beads will depend on the form and the size of the netting units. The connecting beads must be equally spaced.

Pick up a unit of beads and pass the needle through a bead in the base that will provide the distance needed to form half a diamond.

To move to the next row, pass the needle down through the first beads of the row that is ending, exiting the connector bead. You are now ready to begin the next row.

Pick up a unit of beads and attach them to the connector bead in the previous row. Continue around in this manner.

Chevron Chain

The chevron is a simple stitch. Essentially, it consists of picking up beads and going back through one bead in the previous set, creating the characteristic V shapes. Vary the chevron by changing the bead count, the bead shape, and the color placement.

Figure 9. String one bead on the thread and loop through it again, leaving a 6-inch (15 cm) tail. Add nine more beads for a total of 10. To help keep your place, use seven of one color and three of another on this trial run.

Figure 10. Pass the needle through beads #1, #2, #3, and #4 again.

Figure 11. Pick up three dark beads (#11, #12, #13) and three light beads (#14, #15, #16), and pass the needle through bead #7. Pick up three more dark and three light beads and pass the needle through bead #14. Continue in this manner until the desired length is reached.

It is important to try and keep the tension tight as you weave the chain, or it will look sloppy.

Figure 12. To close the chain, pick up beads A, B, and C and pass the needle through bead #1. Pick up beads D and E, pass through the connecting bead, and pick up beads F, G, and H.

Figure 13. Pass the needle through beads #4, #5, #6, #7, #17, #18, and #19. Tie off between beads several times.

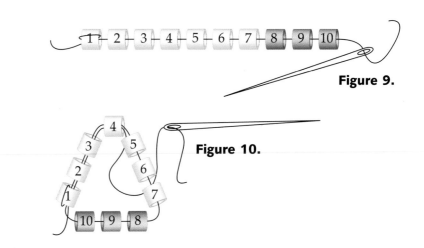

Figure 9.

Figure 10.

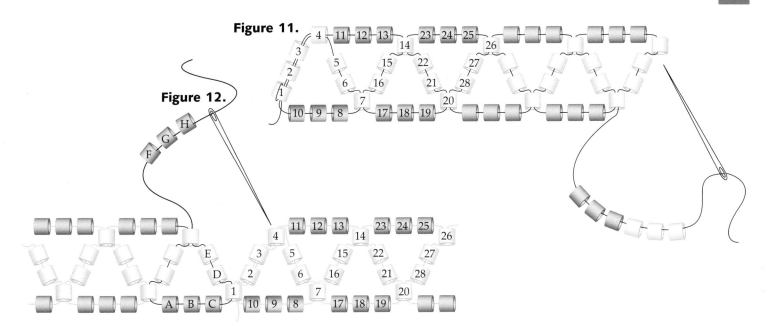

Figure 11.

Figure 12.

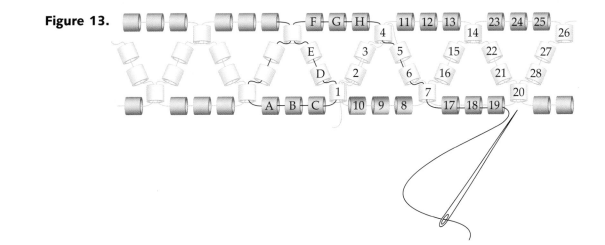

Figure 13.

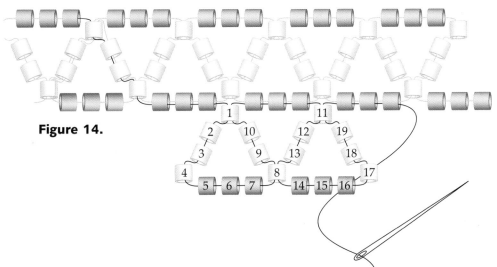

Figure 14.

DOUBLE CHEVRON CHAIN

Figure 14. To widen the chain, exit through one end of a set of edge beads. Pick up 10 beads—four light, three dark, and three light. Pass the needle through bead #1 and another set of edging beads. Add beads #11, #12, and #13 and pass through bead #8. Pick up three dark beads and three light ones, then pass through bead #11 and another set of edge beads. Continue in this manner.

project

Shades of a Different Color

DESIGNER: **NanC Meinhardt**

To create the subtle gradations in this necklace, the designer selected subtle shades of 15 colors for the base beads. For continuity, a black spine was maintained throughout the piece.

MATERIALS

- Beads
  Size 11° glass seed beads:
  - Black, for the spine
  - 15 varying shades that blend well together
  Size 20° glass seed beads
  180 embellishment beads
- Twisted beading thread, tan
- Beading needles
- 1-inch-diameter (2.5 cm) ring, any material
- #10 knitting needle, dowel, or other form

TECHNIQUES USED

✓ African helix
✓ Tubular peyote stitch

FINISHED SIZE

24 inches x 1 inch x ½ inch
(61 x 2.5 x 1.5 cm)

INSTRUCTIONS

1. String on 16 beads in four groups of four, each composed of three of the base color and one of the spine color. Tie into a ring using two square knots.

Slide the ring of beads onto the form so that three base-colored beads are to the left of the knot.

2. Work African helix stitch, using three base-colored beads, one spine-colored bead, and one base-colored bead for each stitch. Change and blend the base color every 2 inches (5 cm) for a total of 32 inches (81.5 cm).

NOTE: Remove the form after about an inch (2.5 cm) of the helix is done; keeping the tension tight seems easier when worked in the hands.

3. Work peyote stitch around the 1-inch (2.5 cm) ring, using the 20° seed beads. Embroider a clump of seed beads onto the outside bottom of the ring. At the bottom of this cluster, make fringes of varying lengths with the embellishment beads, alternating with the spine-colored seed beads to form a tassel that hangs from the clump of beads.

Slide the ring with tassel onto the helix rope.

4. Take out the first row of 16 beads on the helix. This is the only row whose bead count varies from the rest of the necklace. Now the two ends can be joined by lining up the spirals and weaving them together.

NOTE: Because the helix is somewhat fragile in nature, adding additional thread through the spines will give the work added strength.

project

Victorian Lace Collar

DESIGNER: **Jody Stewart-Keller**

Try not to be put off by the length of these instructions! Vertical netting is the easiest type of netting to do, as this nostalgic necklace will demonstrate, if you attempt it. These mighty lists of beads are included in case you want to replicate this necklace exactly. Feel free to create your own variation.

MATERIALS

- Beads

  Size 15° seed beads,
    metallic gold: 15 grams

  Size 13° black charlottes: 2 hanks
    (12-strand, 12-inch [30.5 cm]
    hanks)

  Size 15° hex beads, metallic gold:
    6 grams

  4 mm fire-polished black crystals: 75

  6 mm obsidian beads: 2

- Beading thread, black
- Beading needles, size 13
- Gold lobster claw clasp and
    jump ring

TECHNIQUES USED

✓ Vertical netting

✓ Tubular peyote, odd-count

FINISHED SIZE

11 inches x 10 inches (28 x 25.5 cm)

INSTRUCTIONS

BASE FOR THE NETTING

1. Using odd-count tubular peyote, make a tube nine beads around and 15¾ inches (40 cm) long, using the 15° metallic gold beads. Decrease at each end to close up the tube.

2. With a new thread, string on 342 of the 13° black charlottes; loop through the first bead so they won't fall off. Center the strand along the peyote tube and sew the strand to the tube at every second or third bead, catching the threads between the peyote beads. Keep the strand in a straight line along the tube.

3. Attach a new thread at one end of the tube and weave it through six beads of the anchored strand. Begin the netting.

NETTING

There are 111 rows of netting in this necklace. All are basically the same except for the length of each row and the end treatment. I have tried to simplify the instructions by listing them in a two-column format.

The down column is the beginning half of a row and is read down. The up column is the second half of a row and is read from the bottom up—the same way you are adding the beads. See Figure 1 for an example. At the end of a row, weave through three beads in the base strand and begin the next row. Note that only the hex beads are used as connecting beads.

Figure 2 illustrates the end treatments for the rows. The lists include which ending was used for each row.

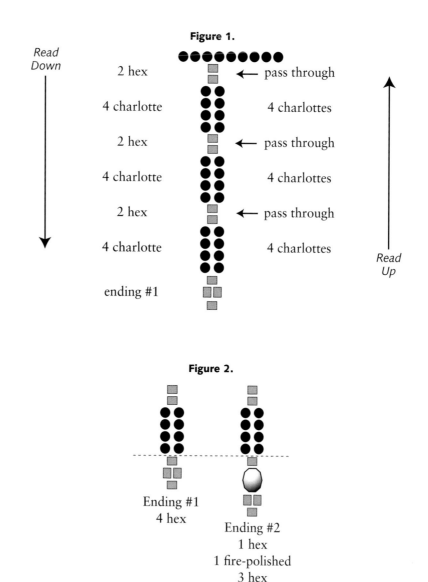

Figure 1.

Read Down

2 hex ← pass through

4 charlotte   4 charlottes

2 hex ← pass through

4 charlotte   4 charlottes

2 hex ← pass through

4 charlotte   4 charlottes

ending #1

Read Up

Figure 2.

Ending #1
4 hex

Ending #2
1 hex
1 fire-polished
3 hex

6 Victorian Lace Collar

Row 1:

DOWN	UP
2 hex	<— pass thru
4 charlottes	4 charlottes
2 hex	2 hex
4 charlottes	4 charlottes
2 hex	<— pass thru
4 charlottes	4 charlottes
ending #1	

Row 2—11:

DOWN	UP
2 hex	<— pass thru
4 charlottes	4 charlottes
<— pass thru	2 hex
4 charlottes	4 charlottes
2 hex	<— pass thru
4 charlottes	4 charlottes
2 hex	2 hex
4 charlottes	4 charlottes
2 hex	<— pass thru
4 charlottes	4 charlottes

Rows 2, 3, 4, 6, 7, 8, 10, 11: ending #1

Rows: 5 & 9: ending #2

Row 12—16:

DOWN	UP
2 hex	<— pass thru
4 charlottes	4 charlottes
<— pass thru	2 hex
4 charlottes	4 charlottes
2 hex	<— pass thru
4 charlottes	4 charlottes
<— pass thru	2 hex
4 charlottes	4 charlottes
2 hex	<— pass thru
4 charlottes	4 charlottes
2 hex	<— pass thru
4 charlottes	4 charlottes

Rows 12, 14, 15, 16: ending #1

Row 13: ending #2

Row 17—20:

DOWN	UP
2 hex	<— pass thru
4 charlottes	4 charlottes
<— pass thru	2 hex
4 charlottes	4 charlottes
2 hex	<— pass thru
4 charlottes	4 charlottes
<— pass thru	2 hex
4 charlottes	4 charlottes
2 hex	<— pass thru
4 charlottes	4 charlottes
2 hex	2 hex
4 charlottes	4 charlottes
2 hex	<— pass thru
4 charlottes	4 charlottes

Rows 18 - 20: ending #1

Row 17: ending #2

Row 21 - 35:

DOWN	UP
2 hex	<— pass thru
4 charlottes	4 charlottes
<— pass thru	2 hex
4 charlottes	4 charlottes
2 hex	<— pass thru
4 charlottes	4 charlottes
<— pass thru	2 hex
4 charlottes	4 charlottes
2 hex	<— pass thru
4 charlottes	4 charlottes
2 hex	2 hex
4 charlottes	4 charlottes
2 hex	<— pass thru
4 charlottes	4 charlottes
2 hex	2 hex
4 charlottes	4 charlottes
2 hex	<— pass thru
4 charlottes	4 charlottes

Rows 22 - 24: ending #1

Rows 21, 25 - 35: ending #2

Row 36—42:

DOWN	UP
2 hex	<— pass thru
4 charlottes	4 charlottes
<— pass thru	2 hex
4 charlottes	4 charlottes
2 hex	<— pass thru
4 charlottes	4 charlottes
<— pass thru	2 hex
4 charlottes	4 charlottes
2 hex	<— pass thru
4 charlottes	4 charlottes
2 hex	2 hex
4 charlottes	4 charlottes
2 hex	<— pass thru
4 charlottes	4 charlottes
2 hex	2 hex
4 charlottes	4 charlottes
2 hex	<— pass thru
4 charlottes	4 charlottes

Rows 36 - 42: ending #2

Row 43—49:

DOWN	UP
2 hex	<— pass thru
4 charlottes	4 charlottes
<— pass thru	2 hex
4 charlottes	4 charlottes
2 hex	<— pass thru
4 charlottes	4 charlottes
<— pass thru	2 hex
4 charlottes	4 charlottes
2 hex	<— pass thru
4 charlottes	4 charlottes
2 hex	2 hex
4 charlottes	4 charlottes
2 hex	<— pass thru
4 charlottes	4 charlottes
2 hex	2 hex
4 charlottes	4 charlottes
2 hex	<— pass thru
4 charlottes	4 charlottes
2 hex	2 hex
4 charlottes	4 charlottes
2 hex	<— pass thru
4 charlottes	4 charlottes
2 hex	2 hex
4 charlottes	4 charlottes
2 hex	<— pass thru
4 charlottes	4 charlottes

Rows 43 - 49: ending #2

Row 50—52:

DOWN	UP
2 hex	<— pass thru
4 charlottes	4 charlottes
<— pass thru	2 hex
4 charlottes	4 charlottes
2 hex	<— pass thru
4 charlottes	4 charlottes
<— pass thru	2 hex
4 charlottes	4 charlottes
2 hex	<— pass thru
4 charlottes	4 charlottes
2 hex	2 hex
4 charlottes	4 charlottes
2 hex	<— pass thru
4 charlottes	4 charlottes
2 hex	2 hex
4 charlottes	4 charlottes
2 hex	<— pass thru
4 charlottes	4 charlottes
2 hex	2 hex
4 charlottes	4 charlottes
2 hex	<— pass thru
4 charlottes	4 charlottes
2 hex	2 hex
4 charlottes	4 charlottes
2 hex	<— pass thru
4 charlottes	4 charlottes

Row 50 - 52: ending #2

Row 53—54: The endings are a little different on these two rows. Repeat row #52 and end it with 3 hex, 1 fire-polished, 3 hex for row #53. For row #54 again repeat row #52 and end like this: 7 hex, 1 fire-polished, 3 hex.

Row 55: Repeat row #52 and add:

2 hex	2 hex
4 charlottes	4 charlottes
2 hex	<— pass thru
4 charlottes	4 charlottes
ending #2	

Row 56: The longest row and the center front row: repeat row #55 changing the end to 4 hex, 1 fire-polished, 3 hex.

Repeat rows 55 thru 1 counting backwards.

If the thread runs out while you are weaving the netting, tie off in the peyote tube, add another thread, and continue.

FINISHING

To finish the piece, weave into the peyote tube and have the needle exit at one end. Add a 6 mm obsidian bead, a fire-polished bead, and seven to nine metallic gold beads. Loop around the finding and pass the needle through the fire-polished and obsidian beads; weave into the tube. Weave from the tube to the finding and back about five times to insure strength. Repeat this process on the other end.

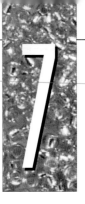

7

Combining Stitches

The art of using multiple stitches is certainly not a new one, but it has never been more popular. Many of the pieces in the gallery move from one stitch to another and often to yet another, adding interest and variety to the piece. A chapter about these transformations seemed appropriate. It would be best to gain a good working knowledge of each individual stitch before trying to combine them.

 MARLA SKOLNIK

Surprises,

vessel, 5 in. x 5 in. diameter (12.5 cm x 12.5 cm), peyote stitch, right-angle weave, brick stitch, and surface embellishment, 11° seed beads and other assorted beads.

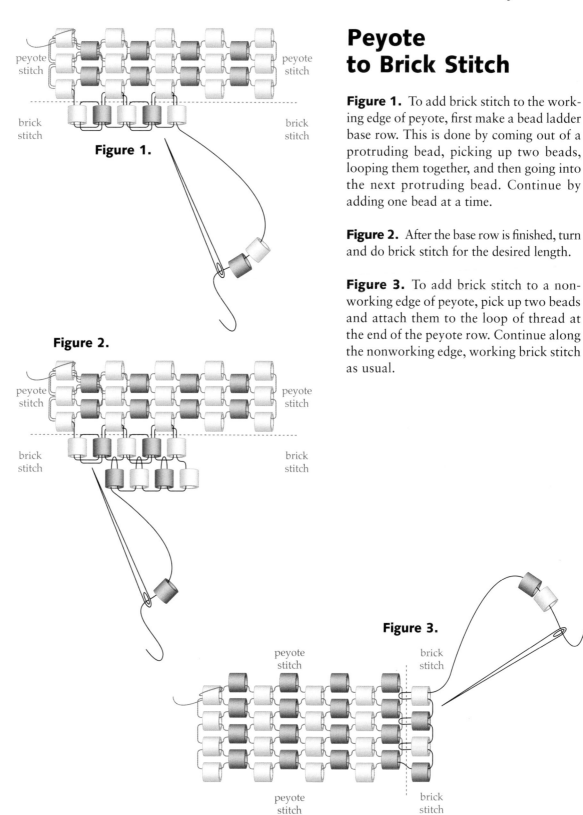

peyote stitch · peyote stitch

brick stitch · brick stitch

Figure 1.

Figure 2.

peyote stitch · peyote stitch

brick stitch · brick stitch

Figure 3.

peyote stitch · brick stitch

peyote stitch · brick stitch

Peyote to Brick Stitch

Figure 1. To add brick stitch to the working edge of peyote, first make a bead ladder base row. This is done by coming out of a protruding bead, picking up two beads, looping them together, and then going into the next protruding bead. Continue by adding one bead at a time.

Figure 2. After the base row is finished, turn and do brick stitch for the desired length.

Figure 3. To add brick stitch to a nonworking edge of peyote, pick up two beads and attach them to the loop of thread at the end of the peyote row. Continue along the nonworking edge, working brick stitch as usual.

LIZ MANFREDINI

Naked Angel,

sculpture,
8¼ in. x 4 in. x 2¾ in.
(21 cm x 10 cm x 7 cm),
peyote stitch
(body and base),
square stitch
(wings),
11° seed beads.

PHOTO:
Joe Manfredini

Peyote to Square Stitch

Figure 4. To add square stitch to the working edge of peyote stitch, exit any bead and string on the number of beads needed for the width of the square stitch unit. Begin square stitch, working back toward the peyote piece, keeping the beads as close to the peyote section as possible.

Figure 5. When the last bead of the second row of square stitch is done, pass the needle through the next protruding peyote bead and continue with square stitch. A gap will form between the recessed peyote beads and the square stitch.

Figure 6. To add square stitch to a nonworking edge, pick up the number of beads needed for the width desired. Begin square stitch and work the row until you reach the peyote section. Pass the needle through the peyote bead, down into the peyote bead below, and through all the square stitch beads already added. Loop up and through the next peyote bead and begin the square stitch again.

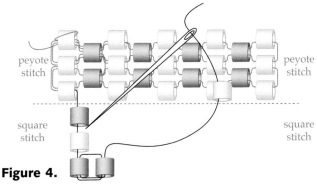

peyote stitch · peyote stitch

square stitch · square stitch

Figure 4.

peyote stitch · peyote stitch

gap

square stitch · square stitch

Figure 5.

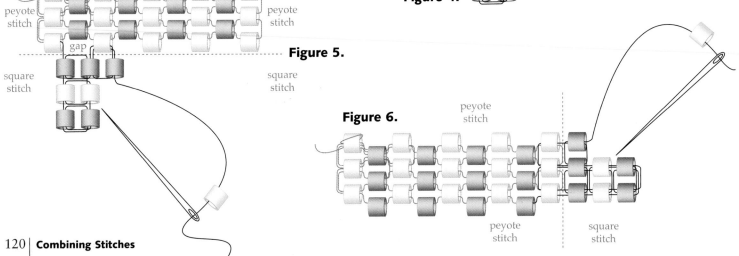

Figure 6.

peyote stitch

peyote stitch · square stitch

Peyote to Right-Angle Weave

Figure 7. To add right-angle weave to peyote stitch, pick up four beads at the beginning of a peyote row and use the first bead strung on as the base peyote bead. Loop around and back through this bead and finish the peyote stitch.

In the next stitch, pick up three beads and pass through bead #2, the connecting right-angle bead, bead #5, the first bead put on in this stitch, and the peyote base. Continue across in this manner.

Figure 8. When you reach the end of the row, weave into position to start another row of right-angle weave.

NOTE: If you want the piece to be symmetrical, you will need to start from odd-count flat peyote. This will give you protruding beads on both sides to work from.

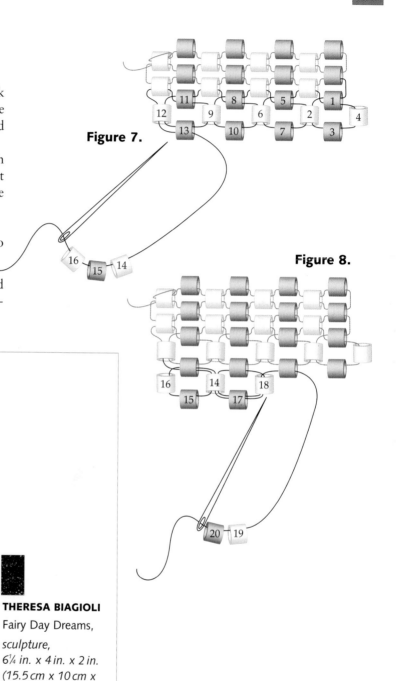

Figure 7.

Figure 8.

THERESA BIAGIOLI
Fairy Day Dreams,
sculpture,
6¼ in. x 4 in. x 2 in.
(15.5 cm x 10 cm x 5 cm), tubular peyote stitch (body), peyote ruffle (skirt), right-angle weave (wings and grass), tubular brick stitch (tree), twisted fringe (leaves and hair), and surface embellishment.

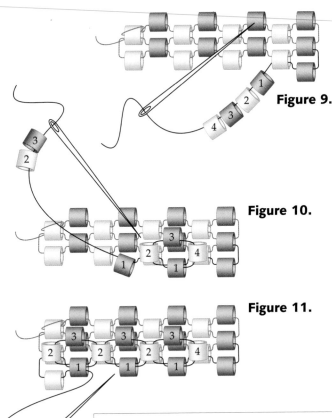

Figure 9.

Figure 10.

Figure 11.

Peyote With Right-Angle Weave Surface Embellishment

While you are doing peyote stitch, you can add right-angle weave on top of the peyote base. You can then build from this to form three-dimensional works or just use it to add texture.

Figure 9. Pick up four beads; bead #1 will form the base peyote bead. Pass the needle back through bead #1, forming a ring of beads, and through the next bead in the peyote base.

Figure 10. Pick up three beads and pass the needle through bead #2 in the previous ring, bead #1 of this set, and the next bead in the peyote base.

Figure 11. This illustration shows the row completed and a regular row of peyote being worked.

NANC MEINHARDT
Fable Vessel, *8 in. x 16 in. x 10 in. (20.5 cm x 40.5 x 25.5 cm),*
brick stitch, peyote stitch, right-angle weave, surface embellishment
with beads, and silk thread embroidery, 11° seed beads and other assorted beads.

Brick Stitch to Peyote Stitch

Figure 12. Weaving in and out of the last row of brick stitch, add beads to the working edge. They will lie perpendicular to the brick stitch beads and between the vertical rows.

After adding the last bead needed to achieve the width desired, pick up a bead. Moving in the opposite direction, work peyote stitch across the row.

Figure 13. The nonworking edge of brick stitch looks exactly like a working edge of peyote stitch and can be used as such. This illustration shows how easily the transition can be.

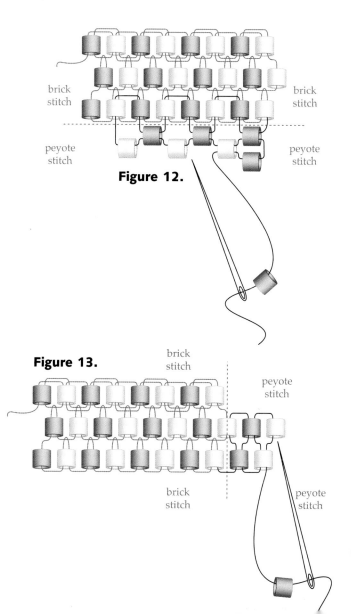

brick stitch

brick stitch

peyote stitch

peyote stitch

Figure 12.

Figure 13.

brick stitch

peyote stitch

brick stitch

peyote stitch

brick stitch

peyote stitch

CONSTANCE GAÂL ROSE

Bracelet and Neckpiece with Turquoise,

2 in. x 7 in. x ¼ in. (5 cm x 18 cm x .5 cm) and 11 in. x 2¼ in. x ¼ in. (28 cm x 5.5 cm x .5 cm), brick stitch with peyote stitch bezels, 11° seed beads, turquoise, and freshwater pearls.

Earrings With Turquoise,

4 in. x ¾ in. x ¼ in. (10 cm x 2 cm x .5 cm), brick stitch with peyote stitch bezels, 11° seed beads, turquoise and freshwater pearls.

Brick Stitch to Square Stitch

Figure 14. To add square stitch to the working edge of brick stitch, exit any bead and string on the number of beads needed for the width of the square stitch section. Begin square stitch, working back toward the brick stitch piece.

Figure 15. When the last bead of the second row of square stitch is done, pass the needle into the corresponding brick stitch bead, back down the first row of square stitch (including the brick stitch bead), and back up the second row. This helps to reinforce the work. Go down through the adjacent brick stitch bead and begin square stitch row three.

Adding square stitch to the nonworking edge of brick is done the same way as adding square stitch to the working edge of peyote stitch.

CAROL WILCOX WELLS
Under the Apple Tree,

brooch, 6 in. x 1½ in. x ¼ in. (15 cm x 4 cm x .5 cm),
peyote stitch with surface embellishment, peyote spikes,
and right-angle weave, 11° cylinder seed beads, 15° seed beads,
other assorted beads, and a twig from an apple tree.

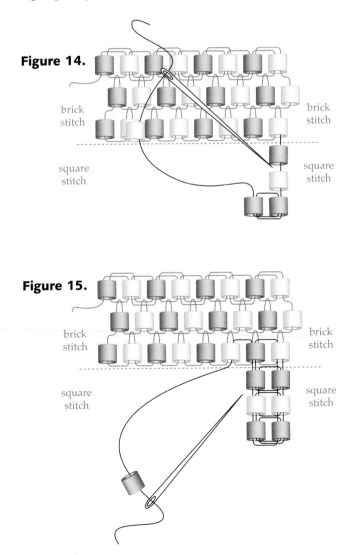

Figure 14.

brick stitch · brick stitch

square stitch · square stitch

Figure 15.

brick stitch · brick stitch

square stitch · square stitch

Brick Stitch to Right-Angle Weave

Figure 16. Exiting a bead on the working edge of brick stitch, pick up a bead and weave into the next bead in the brick row. Pass the needle down into the next bead; pick up another bead and attach it in the same manner. Add as many beads as needed. These beads are the base row for the right-angle weave.

Loop around the last two brick beads and back through the end base bead. Pick up three beads. Pass the needle through the base bead, through the three beads again, and into the next base bead. Continue with right-angle weave.

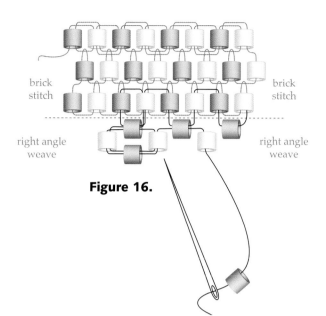

brick stitch

brick stitch

right angle weave

right angle weave

Figure 16.

JOANN BAUMANN
Harlequin Hat Dance,
*basket, 2½ in. x 6¼ in.
(6.5 cm x 15.5 cm),
brick stitch and netting,
assorted glass beads
and Baumann's
lampworked beads.*

Square Stitch to Peyote

Figure 17. Coming out of a square stitch piece on the side, pick up a bead and pass the needle through the next square stitch bead. Pick up another bead and continue doing peyote across the row.

Because the square stitch is so tight, the peyote beads cannot move into their regular positions on the first row.

Figure 18. The second row will look pretty much the same; it won't be until the third row that the vertical brick pattern of the peyote stitch is evident. This third row will also cause small gaps to appear.

Figure 19. If you plan in advance and add an edging bead every other row to a piece of square stitch, you can use those beads as the first row of peyote stitch on the nonworking edge. They can also be added later.

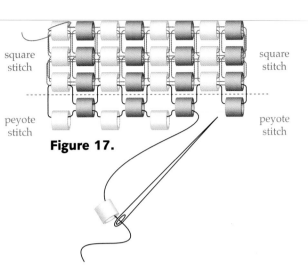

Figure 17.

Figure 18.

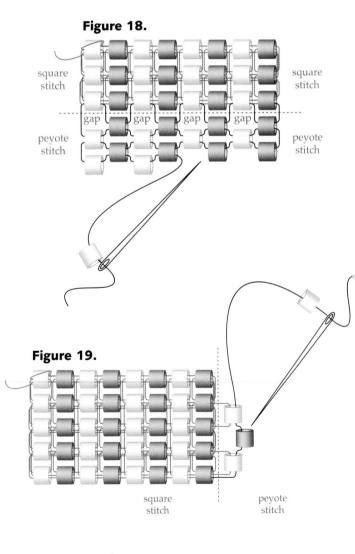

Figure 19.

JOYCE SCOTT
The Gatherer,

12 in. x 8 in. x 5 in. (30.5 cm x 20.5 cm x 12.5 cm); single, two-, and three-drop peyote stitch and netting on wire and thread; 5°, 6°, 10°, and 12° glass seed beads, and a stone.

PHOTO: Kanji Takeno

Square Stitch to Brick Stitch

Figure 20. Coming out of a square stitch piece on the side, pick up two beads and pass the needle under and over the threads between the last two beads of the square stitch row.

Figure 21. After passing the needle through the brick stitch bead, pick up another bead and catch the threads between the next set of square stitch beads.

Figure 22. You can also do the brick stitch right off of the vertical edge, using the side connecting threads to attach the beads.

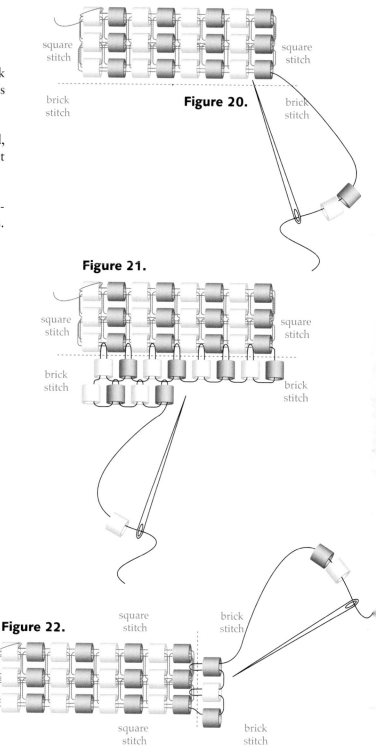

square stitch · square stitch

brick stitch · **Figure 20.** · brick stitch

Figure 21.

square stitch · square stitch

brick stitch · brick stitch

Figure 22. · square stitch · brick stitch

square stitch · brick stitch

LIZ MANFREDINI
Handkerchief Vase,

*7 in. x 3¾ in. x 3¾ in. (18 x 9.5 cm x 9.5 cm),
peyote over a glass vase, right-angle weave
(netting and handkerchiefs), 11° seed beads.*
PHOTO: Joe Manfredini

■ **NANC MEINHARDT**
Flying Across the Tasman Sea, *amulet purse, 4 in. x 3 in. x ¾ in. (10 cm x 7.5 cm x 2 cm), peyote stitch and right angle weave, 11° seed beads and other assorted beads.*

Square Stitch to Right-Angle Weave

Figure 23. Adding right-angle weave to the working edge of square stitch is done by weaving a bead onto every other vertical row and using those beads as one point in the right-angle weave stitch.

Exiting the last bead added, pick up three beads and weave back through all the beads and into the next base bead. Continue with right-angle weave.

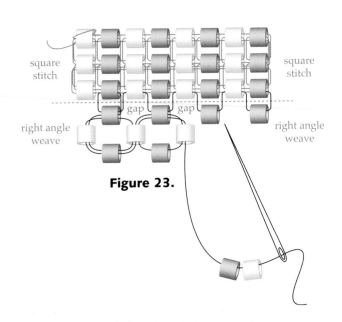

square stitch   square stitch

gap   gap

right angle weave   right angle weave

Figure 23.

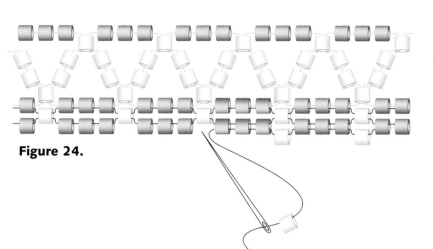

Figure 24.

Chevron Chain to Peyote

Figure 24. The chevron chain provides the perfect edge for peyote stitch. The easiest way is to add a single bead between each set of edging beads for the first row and then work three-drop peyote for the next row.

Figure 25. You could also go into all single peyote, but the middle bead of each chevron edging set would distort a little bit.

Figure 25.

CAROL WILCOX WELLS
Green and Black Basket,
*7 in. x 4¾ in. diameter
(18 cm x 12 cm),
chevron chain, peyote
stitch (single, two-, three-,
four-, and five-drop),
11° and 15° seed beads,
4 mm fire-polished beads.*

project

Cuffed Basket

DESIGNER: **Carol Wilcox Wells**

When I first started playing with the chevron chain, I immediately saw the possibilities of including peyote stitch. This led to much experimentation and finally to one of my favorite baskets.

MATERIALS

- Beads

  Size 11° seed beads

    Transparent rainbow topaz:
    20 grams

    Matte amethyst iridescent:
    9 grams

    Matte emerald iridescent:
    5 grams

- Beading thread, gray
- Beading needles, size 12

TECHNIQUES USED

✓ Chevron chain

✓ Combining chevron chain with peyote stitch

✓ Tubular peyote, even-count

✓ Increasing and decreasing

FINISHED SIZE

2¼ inch x 2 inches x 2 inches
(6 x 5 x 5 cm)

INSTRUCTIONS

1. Make a chevron chain 17 sets long, using the topaz beads for the edging and the amethyst for the inside beads. Close the chain.

2. Using the above as a base, add another row of chevron (see the instructions for a double chevron). This time use the matte green beads for the inside color and continue the topaz as the edging.

3. Do two more rows of the chevron, alternating the inside colors. When you are finished you will have a quadruple chevron chain. This will become the cuffed top of the basket.

4. Begin the body of the basket, switching from chevron chain to peyote. Work the body in even-count tubular peyote, using the following sequence of stitches and colors.

All of the rows that are single beads will use the matte amethyst bead, creating a narrow stripe.

- The two, three, and four-drop rows use the transparent rainbow topaz beads.
- The five-drop row has two topaz, one matte green, and two topaz as its color lineup.
- The row sequence is as follows:
- 7 rows of single and three-drop peyote, beginning and ending with a single row.

NOTE: These are seven rows counting on the diagonal; for one row, you will weave once around the basket in single peyote and for the next row once around in three-drop, alternating stitches.

- 7 rows of four-drop and single peyote, beginning and ending with a four-drop row.
- 17 rows of single and five-drop peyote, beginning and ending with a single row.
- 7 rows of four-drop and single peyote, beginning and ending with a four-drop row.
- 5 rows of single and three-drop peyote, beginning and ending with a single row.
- 3 rows of two-drop and single peyote, beginning and ending with a two-drop row.
- 5 rows of single peyote, and then decrease as necessary to close up the bottom. Keep the color pattern going so the stripes converge in the center.

5. Fold half of the quadruple chevron chain down to form the inverted cuff.

project

Dimensional Brooch

DESIGNER: **Carol Wilcox Wells**

As a teacher, I am always looking for new ways to teach techniques without ending up with a lot of small samples of beadwork. This brooch uses seven—count them—seven techniques and is known by my students (affectionately, I hope) as "the brooch from hell."

MATERIALS

- Beads

  Size 11° cylinder seed beads

  Black opaque: 1 gram

  Lined light sea foam: .5 gram

  Matte metallic sea foam green: .5 gram

  Matte metallic light aqua: 1 gram

  Size 15° round seed beads

  Black opaque: 1.5 grams

  Lined moss green: .5 gram

  Trim Beads

  2 mm gold-filled: 82

  4 mm onyx: 2

  5 mm turquoise: 16

- 2-inch (5 cm) head pin
- Beading thread, black
- Beading needles, size 12
- 1-inch (2.5 cm) pin finding
- Epoxy and ultrasuede (optional)

TECHNIQUES USED

✓ Flat peyote (odd-count) in single, two-drop, and three-drop

✓ Decreasing on outside edge

✓ Peyote spikes

✓ Fringe

✓ Horizontal netting

FINISHED SIZE

2½ x 2 x ½ inches (6.5 x 5 x 1 cm)

INSTRUCTIONS

Using the colors listed above, arrange the cylinder beads so that the piece takes on the look of turquoise.

1. String on one bead and loop back through it, leaving a good 8-inch (20.5 cm) tail. Add 29 more beads for a total of 30.

2. Turn and do odd-count, two-drop flat peyote back and forth across the piece for a total of eight rows, counting on the diagonal.

3. Decrease on outside edge by two stitches at beginning of row 9, and decrease by two stitches at end of row 9. There will now be 11 vertical rows instead of 15.

4. Do 13 more rows, counting on the diagonal, for a total of 14 rows at this width.

5. On the 15th row, begin increasing by doing three-drop peyote. Keep the tension tight and continue for a total of eight rows, counting on the diagonal.

6. Now start decreasing by switching to two-drop peyote; work two-drop for a total of eight rows, counting on the diagonal. Remember to keep the tension tight. The increasing and decreasing plus the tension will form the bulge in the fabric of the beads.

7. Decrease again by switching to single peyote; work two rows, counting on the diagonal.

8. On the next row, alternate one single-peyote stitch with one peyote spike. Then do a row of single peyote to secure the previous row.

9. Continue adding spike rows and regular rows for a total of 14. You may put on as many or as few spikes as you like. Use two of the turquoise beads here.

10. Now, decreasing on the outside edges, bring these 11 vertical rows to a point.

11. Add fringe to each of the 11 vertical rows as follows:

- Vertical rows 1, 3, 5, 7, 9, and 11: 15° seed bead, cylinder bead, 2 mm gold bead, cylinder bead, 15° seed bead, 5 mm turquoise bead, 2 mm gold bead.

- Vertical rows 2, 4, 8, and 10: 15° seed bead, cylinder bead, 2 mm gold bead, cylinder bead, 15° seed bead, cylinder bead, 2 mm gold bead, cylinder bead, 15° seed bead, 5 mm turquoise bead, 2 mm gold bead.

- Vertical row 6: 15° seed bead, cylinder bead, 2 mm gold bead, cylinder bead, 15° seed bead, cylinder bead, 2 mm gold bead, cylinder bead, 15° seed bead, cylinder bead, 2 mm gold bead, cylinder bead, 15° seed bead, 5 mm turquoise bead, 2 mm gold bead.

12. Go back up to the beginning of the brooch and unloop the thread from around the first bead. Using this thread and the initial eight rows, you will form the casing for the head pin. To do this, weave the tail thread through the first two beads (vertical row 1). Then, counting down four beads in vertical row 2, pass the needle through those two beads. Now go back up to the top of vertical row 3 and go through those beads (see Figure 1). Continue across, pulling the thread tight as you weave along. Don't wait till you get to the end of the row to tighten the thread, or you won't be able to.

13. Slide an onyx bead onto the head pin and thread the head pin through the casing of beads. This may take a little wiggling and pushing, but it will fit. Put the other onyx bead on the head pin, and bend the pin down at a right angle to hold the bead on. Cut the head pin as close to the bead as possible. File the end of the head pin so that it is smooth.

NETTING

The netting is done on the back side of the brooch, using the 15° black seed beads and the 2 mm gold filled beads. The gold beads are numbered to help you see which way to go.

14. Following Figure 2, add a new thread and bring the needle out of the bead marked A heading left. Now pick up 4 black beads, 1 gold bead (#1), 4 black beads, 1 gold (#2), 4 black, 1 gold (#3), and 4 black. Pass the needle through the beads marked C and D. Pick up 4 black, 1 gold (#4), 4 black, and pass the needle through the beads marked E and F. Continue across as shown on the diagram.

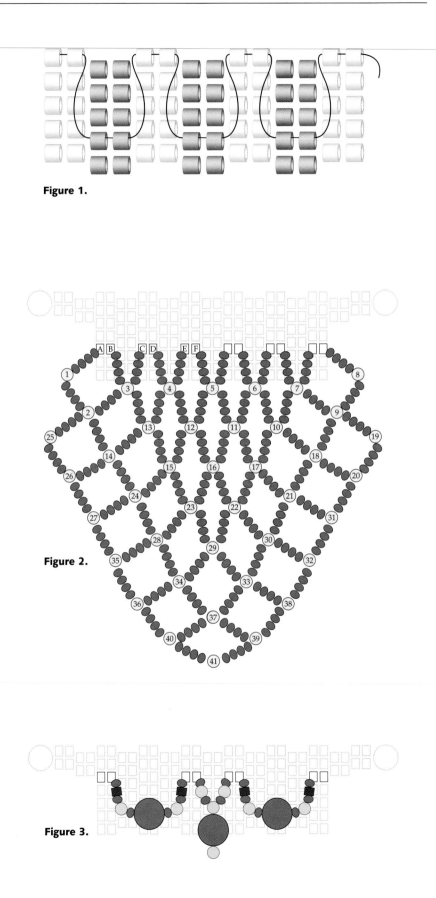

Figure 1.

Figure 2.

Figure 3.

15. When you get to the end of the row, pick up 4 black, 1 gold (#8), 4 black, 1 gold (#9), and 4 black. Turn and pass the needle through gold bead #7. Continue across with 4 black, 1 gold, 4 black until you exit gold bead #3. Pick up 4 black beads, pass the needle through beads B, A, 4 black, gold #1, 4 black, and gold #2.

16. Begin the next row by picking up 4 black, 1 gold (#14), and 4 black. Pass the needle through gold #13. Continue with sets of 4, 1, 4 all the way across. To make the turn pick up 4, 1, 4, 1, 4 and pass the needle into gold #18. Work across to the other side, ending with the needle coming out of gold bead #14.

17. Because the netting begins to decrease on the outside edges, you will have to weave through other beads to turn around and go back the opposite way. At times the thread will have to bypass a gold connecting bead because the opening is in a horizontal position and the direction needed is vertical. The turns on both sides will now require weaving through other beads to get into position to go the opposite way.

Pass the needle through the 4 black beads and gold bead #2. Now pick up 4 black, 1 gold (#25), 4 black, 1 gold (#26), 4 black. Weave through gold #14, 4 black, bypass gold #13, 4 black, gold #3, 4 black, gold #2, 4 black, gold #25, 4 black, and gold #26. Now continue across picking up 4 black, 1 gold, 4 black, ending with the thread exiting gold bead #20. Weave through 4 black, gold #19, 4 black, gold #9, 4 black, bypass gold #18, 4 black, bypass gold #20, 4 black, and gold #31. The needle is now in position to begin the next row.

18. Continue adding beads in this manner, using Figure 2 as a guide. Tie the thread off within the netting.

19. Add the trim beads to the upper front of the brooch as shown in Figure 3.

20. Attach the pin finding to the back of the brooch just above the netting. It can be sewn into place or glued with a two-part epoxy; cover the pin back with a piece of suede, or imitation suede. Take as much care with this process as with the beading of the brooch.

project

The Gilded Cage

DESIGNER:
Carol Wilcox Wells

This amulet purse is a study in form; with a single color, the shapes and textures are very apparent. The graph for the body of the purse is a regular peyote graph until row 61, where the stepped decreasing begins. As beads are eliminated on the actual work, they are also eliminated on the graph, and gaps between vertical rows appear. There will not be any gaps in the actual work except at the point of decrease. Use a straightedge across the graph to help you keep on track.

MATERIALS

- Beads
  Size 11° gilded gold
  cylinder seed beads,
  22 kt: 50 grams

- Beading needles, size 12
- Beading thread, gold
- Cardboard toilet-tissue tube
- Transparent tape

TECHNIQUES USED

✓ Tubular peyote, even-count
✓ Decreasing
✓ Peyote ruffle
✓ Surface embellishment
✓ Netting

FINISHED SIZE

4¾ x 2 x 2 inches ·
  (12 x 5 x 5 cm)

INSTRUCTIONS

BODY OF THE PURSE

1. Thread the needle with about 3 feet (.9 m) of thread. String on 80 beads (dummy rows 1 and 2) and tie into a ring, leaving a two-bead space of thread showing in the finished ring. This amulet purse requires a tighter tension to hold up the exterior netting.

2. Cut the toilet tissue tube in half lengthwise, roll it up, and slide the ring of beads onto the tube. Let the tube expand to the size of the ring of beads. Tape both ends of the tube and up the seam. It is important that both ends of the tube are the same diameter. Roll the ring of beads to within an inch (2.5 cm) of the top of the tube. Tape the tail end of the thread out of the way.

3. Doing even-count tubular peyote, put on one more dummy row for a total of three (these will be taken off later). Add 60 more rows, counting on the diagonal. The red dot on the graph (Figure 1) indicates the first bead of each row.

4. Remove the three false rows before you begin the bottom of the purse. Slide the work down to the lower edge of the tube.

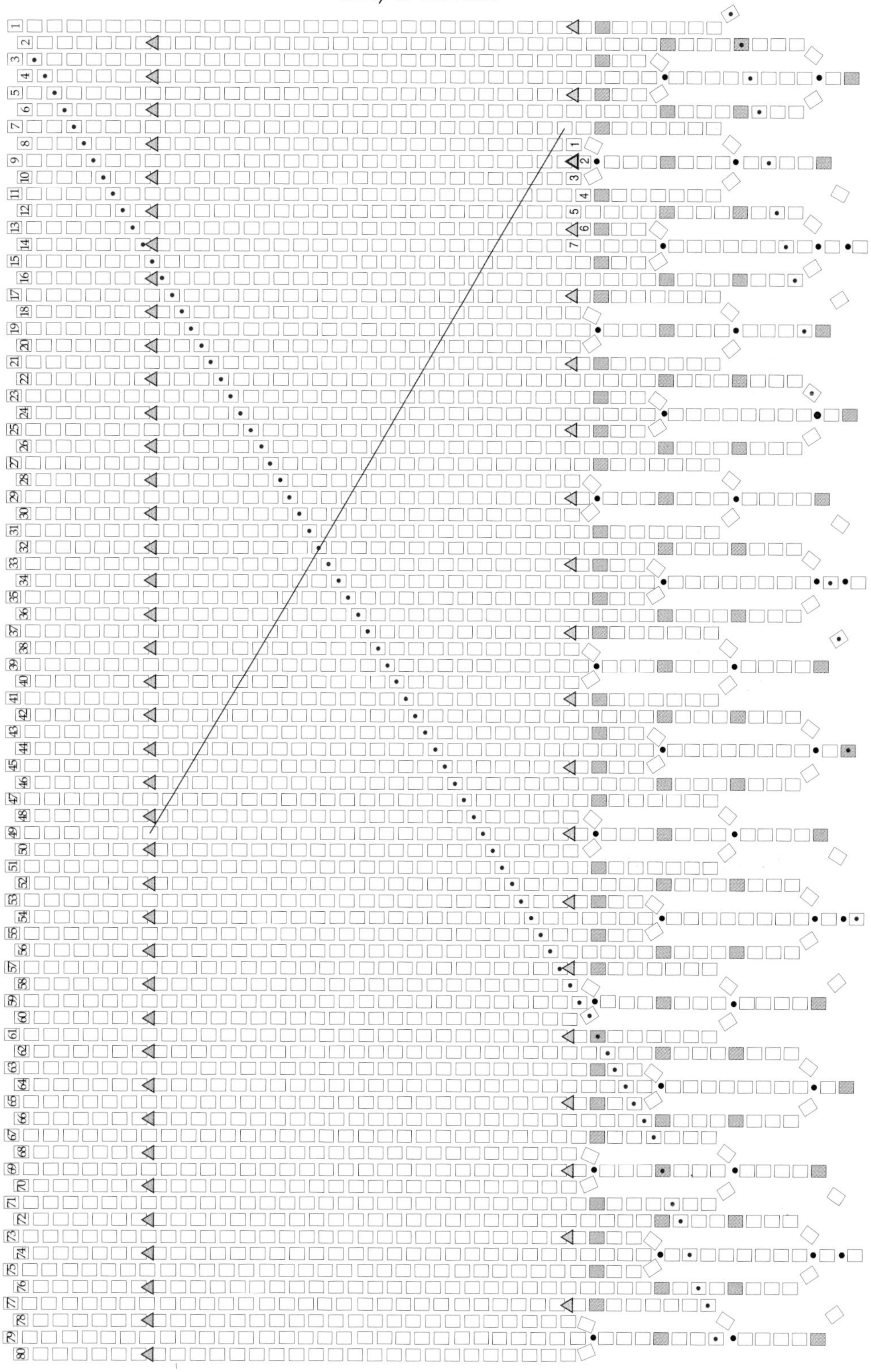

- • 1st bead of each row
- ▨ Decrease row
- • Decrease 1 bead at this marker
- △ Placement of surface embellishment

Figure 1.
Body of the Purse

BOTTOM OF THE PURSE:

When a decrease is made, pull tightly so that the beads come together. For the sake of clarity, the graph shows spaces between the vertical rows; the actual work will not have these spaces. There will be a small V-shaped opening at each point of decrease. These are to be expected and not worried about; they will enhance the design.

5. Row 61, indicated by the light gray squares in Figure 1, is the first row of the bottom and the first row to decrease. Following the graph, put on four beads then decrease by one bead. Do this all the way around the tube. The black dot on the graph indicates the point of decrease.

6. Put on rows 62 through 67. There should be 32 beads per row.

7. Decrease row 68 as shown on the graph.

8. Put on rows 69 through 75. There should be 24 beads per row.

9. Decrease row 76 as shown on the graph.

10. Put on rows 77 through 84. There should be 16 beads per row.

11. Decrease row 85 as shown on the graph.

12. Put on rows 86 through 87. There should be 8 beads per row.

13. Decrease row 88 as shown on the graph.

14. Put on row 89. There should be 4 beads per row. End the thread.

SURFACE EMBELLISHMENT AND NETTING

Looking at the graph in Figure 1, you will see gold triangles along the upper and lower portions of the body of the purse. These show you where to add the first row of surface embellishment beads. It is important that they are in the spaces shown.

15. Find the gold triangle that has the red line around it (third one from the right, bottom row). This is where you will begin. Now, looking at your purse, find the first row of decrease, add a thread near this point, and weave into position #1 shown on the graph. The bead that you will be adding will sit one bead above the actual decrease. Now pick up a bead and pass the needle through bead #3. Weave the thread through beads #4 and #5. Pick up another bead and pass the needle through bead #7. Do this all the way around the bottom of the purse.

16. To do the upper row, weave the needle and thread up the body of the purse 43 rows, counting on the diagonal. Follow the brown line on the graph.

17. The needle will exit the eighth bead from the top, vertical row #49 (see Figure 1). Pick up a bead and go into the eighth bead from the top, vertical row #51. Continue this all the way around the purse. You are doing peyote stitch on the surface, and this is row 1.

18. Now, doing peyote stitch and using the beads that you just put on as the base row, do another row all the way around, for row 2.

19. For row 3, increase every space by one bead (pick up two beads, go into one, pick up two beads, go into one, etc.). This creates a ruffled effect. When you have finished this row, the needle and thread will be coming out of bead

A; see the surface embellishment and netting graph. See Figure 2.

THE NETTING

20. The first row of horizontal netting is done by picking up seven beads and passing the needle through bead C. See Figure 2. Pick up seven more beads and go through bead E. Continue in this manner all the way around the purse.

21. When you get back to bead A, pass the needle and thread through beads #1, #2, #3, and #4 of the first row of netting. You are now ready to begin row 2 of the netting.

22. Pick up seven beads and pass the needle through bead #11 of the first row. Pick up seven more beads and pass the needle through bead #18 of the first row. Continue in this manner all the way around the purse.

23. Do rows 3 through 9 in the same way.

24. Before doing row 10, please study Figures 1 and 2. The beads that you put on the surface of the body of the purse in the positions indicated by the lower set of gold triangles will now be used as the center beads for each loop of netting in row 10. Figure 2 shows five gold triangles in the netting (row 10). The gold triangles (row 10) indicate the position taken within the netting. The netting is longer than the length of the purse. When you use the bead attached to the purse as the center bead for each netting loop, it makes the netting stand out from the body of the purse. Now do row 10 of the netting, attaching it to the bottom of the purse at the gold triangles. Knot and tie off the thread.

Figure 2.
Netting

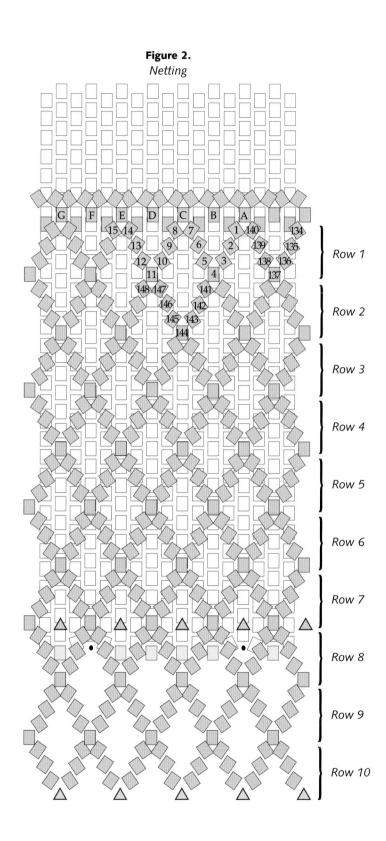

Row 1

Row 2

Row 3

Row 4

Row 5

Row 6

Row 7

Row 8

Row 9

Row 10

FIGURE-EIGHT FRINGE

There is one figure-eight fringe at each decrease point. They are all done in the same way. Begin at the first row of decreases, and work your way around and down the bottom of the purse. See Figure 3 for a diagram of fringe.

25. With the thread coming out of bead A, string on 30 beads. Pass the needle up through bead #10 and put on nine more beads. Now insert the needle into bead B and weave over to the next point of decrease. There are 36 fringes in all.

Figure 3.
Figure Eight Fringe

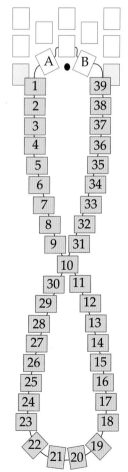

KARRIE JEFFRIES Coming Out, *her interpretation of the Gilded Cage amulet purse, 5½ in. x 2 in. diameter (14 cm x 5 cm), 11° cylinder seed beads and assorted beads.*

THE STRAP

The strap is a beaded chain attached to the ruffle above the netting. See Figure 4.

26. Add a new thread to the top part of the purse. Weave into the first two rows of the surface embellishment beads. The needle should be coming out of bead #2 (Figure 4). Pick up beads #3 through #7 and pass the needle through beads #8, A, #2, #3, #4, and #5. Pick up beads #9 through #15 and pass the needle back through beads #5, #9, #10, #11, and #12. Pick up beads #16 through #22 and pass the needle back through beads #12, #16, #17, #18, and #19. Continue in this manner until the strap is the length needed. Join at the point exactly opposite from where you began the strap. Use the beads in the ruffle as part of the last loop to attach the strap.

THE TOP

27. Follow steps 1 and 2 in these instructions, using 90 beads instead of 80. Add 14 more rows, counting on the diagonal.

28. On row 17, begin the ruffled edge by increasing every stitch by one bead. This is done by picking up two beads and going into one bead, pick up two go into one, all the way around. For row 18 pick up two beads and go into two beads all the way around, being careful to catch all the beads in the proper order. When you have finished, weave to the top of the piece.

29. Slide the unruffled edge of the top to the edge of the tube and start decreasing the same way that you did the bottom of the bag. The only difference will be that you have nine points of decrease instead of eight. This is because you are working with 90 beads instead of 80.

Figure 4.
The Strap

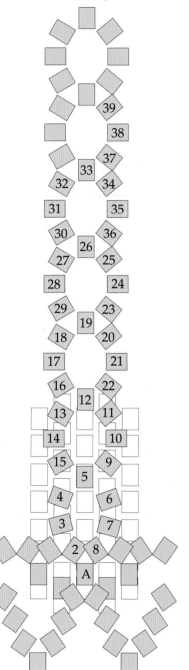

30. Follow the directions for the stepped bottom up to and including row 87, decreasing one extra time in each decrease row because you started with 90 beads.

- The number of beads per row after first decrease should be 36.
- The number of beads per row after the second decrease should be 27.
- The number of beads per row after the third decrease should be 18.
- The number of beads per row after fourth decrease should be 9.

Do seven more rows and then decrease every other stitch. Add one more row of beads to fill in the spaces. Pull tight and knot; weave to bead A on Figure 5.

31. Pick up three beads and go into bead B. Pick up three beads and go into bead C. Do this all the way around. When you reach bead A again, pass the needle up through beads #1 and #2 . Pick up three beads and pass the needle through the middle bead of the last row; continue around. Weave to the top, coming out of bead #17, and pass the needle and thread through beads #20, #23, #26, #29, and #17. Pull tight to close the ring of beads. Tie off and weave into the base before cutting the thread.

32. To attach the top to the purse, make two 20 bead ladders. Sew one to the inside, left side of the purse three rows down, and the other to the right side. Then sew the other end of the left ladder to the inside of the top at the first row of decrease. Do this with the right side as well.

Figure 5.
The Top

Looking down on the last two rows.

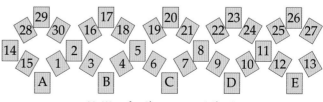

Netting for the crown at the top.

Contributing Artists

JANE A. ALLEY's bead addiction began with a looming class on Whidbey Island, Washington. As an avid RV traveler, she has found that all roads lead to bead stores. Jane has settled in the Mimbres Valley of southwest New Mexico and has a store called A Bead or Two in Silver City.

Before beads took over her life and consumed her soul, **JOANN BAUMANN** was a metalsmith who included beads in her work; now she is a seed bead artist whose work includes metal, her own lampworked beads, and fused glass. JoAnn is captivated by the color and the reflectivity of the beads: "The whole medium has totally seduced me."

THERESA BIAGIOLI moved from the mild, moist Pacific Northwest to hot, arid San Juan, Argentina and found a whole new hemisphere of flora and fauna to be discovered and re-created. Her beadwork tends to reflect memories she wants to preserve.

TINA BLOOMENTHAL is a working bead artist who teaches and shows in the Chicago area. She is represented by the Joy Horwich Gallery. Although she loves beads of all kinds, seed beads allow her to experiment with new techniques, which in turn expand her creativity.

CYNTHIA CUNNINGHAM majored in graphic design in college and has been very involved in polymer clay for the last six or seven years. She has been beading for less than a year, although she has collected beads for over 20 years: "The primary goal of my work is to evoke emotion through the use of color and texture. Nothing more."

BARB DAVIS is a self-taught beadwork artist. She began loom beading 10 years ago and has expanded her skills to include 15 more techniques. Most widely known for her beaded animal skulls, she shows and sells her work throughout the United States and Canada.

WENDY ELLSWORTH began her career in the early 1970s doing commission work in seed bead mandalas that were incorporated into women's purses. Since 1990, she has focused on sculptural forms and, more recently, beaded baskets and vessels. Her studio is in Buck's County, Pennsylvania.

Coming from generations of Appalachian craftsmen, **LINDA FIFIELD** finds commitment to a creative life quite natural. Fifteen years of experimentation with beaded baskets have led her to value equally the form, which she turns on a lathe, the pattern, the colors, and the control of the beading technique.

MARLA GASSNER has worked with beads most of her life. Her designs evolve around found objects and beads. Some of her favorites are ivory, bone, turquoise, coral, amethyst, jade, and antique crystals. Marla's work can be seen in exclusive boutiques throughout the Chicago area.

ANN GEISERT discovered beads and off-loom techniques while looking for a way to survive Chicago's long, cold winters. A second generation Polish-American, she draws her inspiration from Polish folk art as well as from the scenes and structures in Chicago.

SUSAN GEISERT is a lifelong resident of the culturally diverse north side of Chicago who discovered beads and beading in a neighborhood bead shop. Her creations reflect her experience with needlepoint, sewing, and stained glass, as well as her unique sense of color.

JULIE GOETSCH has a B.A. and M.A. in Clothing and Textiles from Wayne State University. Formerly a designer and teacher of canvas embroidery and clothing embellishment, she is now focused on beadwork, as a teacher and designer.

LAURA GOLDBERG has been beading for two years: "To me, the satisfaction of beading comes as much from the tactile pleasure of handling the beads as from the array and combination of colors that unfold as the work progresses."

JEANNINE ANDERSON GORESKI received her B.F.A. and M.F.A. from Colorado State University. She is an Assistant Professor of Art at Berea College in Berea, Kentucky. Her baskets are exhibited internationally and featured in several publications.

CATHERINE HARRIS has been creating beaded amulet purses for three years, including "Maui Evening." Drawing on a fine arts background with a three-dimensional emphasis, she currently develops her original designs in her home studio with the aid of a computer.

MERRI BETH HILL has no formal art training, but has experimented with numerous crafts since childhood. Most of her creative energy is focused on stitchery in one form or another, be it beading, embroidery, quilting, or doll making.

KARRIE JEFFRIS has been beading for six years and has recently focused on amulet purses. She has attended national workshops and given demonstrations in Evanston, Illinois, and her work has been published in *Bead & Button* magazine.

Beads and jewelry have fascinated **ELLA JOHNSON-BENTLEY** since childhood. After her retirement in 1984 from commercial fishing, she learned basic beading from a friend. She enjoys color and the details of turning one of her designs into "bead art."

DIANE KARZEN's beadwork is based on her background in drawing, painting, and ceramics. The color, design, and three-dimensional qualities of these media play an important role in her work. The use of beads has opened up a new form of expression and creativity for her.

SUSAN LUTZ KENYON graduated from Barat College and attended The School of the Arts Institute and Arrowmont School of Arts and Crafts. She has been sewing for 28 years and doing beadwork for five. Susan is currently the Program Chair for the Bead Society of Greater Chicago and works as the craft coordinator at a seniors' living facility.

Contributing Artists

LIZ MANFREDINI has worked in many different media, but none captured her heart more than beads. A frequent traveler, Liz is an avid collector of folk art from around the world, and these pieces have provided her with much inspiration. "I love to be surrounded by a riot of color, and that is reflected in my work."

DENEEN MATSON's discovery of off-loom bead weaving two years ago has given "the artist within a voice of its own," with "guidance and inspiration" from her two teachers, Carol Wilcox Wells and NanC Meinhardt. Her current expressions are a series of small-scale, historically based ethnic dresses.

NANC MEINHARDT, an accomplished bead artist, exhibits her work and teaches internationally. She has been published in *Fiberarts Design Book 5*, *Creative Bead Jewelry* by Carol Taylor, and *Bead & Button* magazine. NanC uses beadwork as a vehicle to explore the creative process. She resides in Highland Park, Illinois.

KATHLYN MOSS is a self-taught bead artist and author with a degree in art education. Her passionate interest is to use beaded forms to create not only flat colored surfaces, but dimensional structures as well—and to assemble the various elements into jewelry. She is the coauthor of *The New Beadwork*.

LINDSAY OBERMEYER's art has been exhibited throughout the United States and abroad and has appeared in numerous publications, including *Fiberarts* magazine, *American Craft*, and *The New Beadwork*. Lindsay is owner of The Weaving Workshop, a textile supply store in Chicago. She has an M.F.A. from the University of Washington and a B.F.A. from The School of the Art Institute of Chicago.

ANN WINEBRENNER PAXTON works as a Municipal Court Judge by day and as a bead artist by night. Her work focuses primarily on spiritual themes and was recently exhibited in "Seed Dreams/Beaded Visions" at the University of Minnesota. She lives in San Diego, California, with her musician/composer husband, Jim.

KATHY ROBIN is a relative newcomer to beading. Much of her experience in combining colors, textures, and patterns comes from garden design, where the role of reflected light is as fundamental as it is with beads. Kathy is captivated by the amulet purse: "While creating this bag, both the intense quality of the color and the accompanying sounds of my son's electric guitar inspired the name Electric Blues."

CONSTANCE GAÄL ROSE has a creative background in fibers, textiles, and needle arts. Working with beads was a natural progression. Her work is strongly influenced by art nouveau and art deco designs and by unusual methods of construction.

CYNTHIA RUTLEDGE, who is General Manager of The Shepherdess in San Diego, California, specializes in peyote stitch and off-loom weaving techniques with an emphasis on sculptural shapes. Her work has been exhibited in national juried shows and has appeared in Nicolette Stessin's *Beaded Amulet Purses*, Carol Taylor's *Creative Bead Jewelry*, and *Bead & Button* magazine.

JOYCE SCOTT was "born an artist" in Baltimore, Maryland, and resides there today. She was educated at the Maryland Institute College of Art (B.F.A.), Instituto Allende in Mexico (M.F.A.), Haystack Mountain School of Crafts, and Rochester Institute of Technology. Traditional beadwork, weaving, papermaking, and contemporary theater are a few of her exceptional talents. Her works have been shown in galleries and museums internationally.

KATHY SEELY's background is in painting and fiber arts. In 1993 she took a class in off-loom bead weaving, and beads have been the focus of her work ever since. She loves the way they capture and change light and finds the process of stitching them together one at a time a creative meditation. Kathy lives in Oak Ridge, Tennessee, with her husband, nine cats, and numerous wild creatures in the woods nearby.

MARLA SKOLNIK's designs encompass vast areas of art, always with emphasis on color, texture, form, and detail. As a professional designer with degrees in art and architectural design, she finds that light plays an important part in her projects. The beaded vessel "Surprises" challenged her to create a vessel that would ebb and flow with color enhanced by light.

JODY STEWART-KELLER is a professional bead weaver and designer who lives in Asheville, North Carolina. Her work is exhibited in galleries throughout the U.S. For six years she has been creating ornate jewelry in the off-loom style, using various forms of peyote stitch and tiny size 14° beads.

FRAN STONE retired 14 years ago and took the opportunity to tap into her creative spirit, earning an Associate Degree in Graphic Arts in 1983. The Shepherdess in San Diego introduced her to the world of beads: "Discovering seed beads and off-loom weaving has made my retirement years perhaps the most rewarding part of my life, and I am ever grateful."

MARCIE STONE graduated from the California College of Arts and Crafts in 1974 and has worked as a studio artist since then. Her beadwork has appeared in numerous galleries, collections, and publications. She is perhaps best known for her combinations of jeweled encrustations with pine needle basketry and her beaded neck pieces.

GINI WILLIAMS is a nationally recognized bead artist, best known for her multi-technique, sculptural beadwork. Her works have been exhibited in many museums and galleries and have earned her numerous awards.

Acknowledgments

The entire experience of writing this book was both overwhelming and gratifying. Thanks to the following people who contributed to the process.

Burr and Doris Wilcox, who let me travel my own path with their full support and love always.

Burr McLawhorn, my son, whose life path provided deep-felt inspiration and who can always make me smile.

Aaron McLawhorn, the quiet son, who brings out all of the "mother" in me and who has promised me a trip to the beach in a limo.

Virginia Blakelock and Carol Perrenoud for the beginning elements of off-loom beading.

Robin Hadle, for her "pushing me to do it-ness" and cherished friendship.

Lindsay Obermeyer, for suggesting that I teach a class on peyote stitch and become an active member of the Bead Society of Greater Chicago.

Alice Scherer and The Center for the Study of Beadwork, for her hospitality, for access to the center's resources, and for a wonderful day at the fair.

Valerie Hector, for her willingness to share her expertise in the field of bead research.

NanC Meinhardt, a dear friend, for listening and for her exuding creativity, which she shares worldwide.

All of my students, for asking questions that made me think and for their personal visions, which let me see things in a different way.

Carol Taylor, my editor, for the opportunity and for the deadlines.

All of the contributing artists, for their talent, patience, and willingness to share a part of themselves through a project or a gallery piece in this book. I could not have done it without you and would not have wanted to.

Robert C. Wells Jr., alias Bob, Saint Bob, "I'd love to take your order" Bob, and my sweetie, for providing me with the love and the freedom to let me be me. A man of many talents who got caught in the vortex of beads.

"It is the supreme art of the teacher to awaken joy in creative expression and knowledge."

~Albert Einstein

Bibliography

Barth, Georg J. *Native American Beadwork.* Stevens Point, Wisconsin: R. Schmeider, 1913.

Blakelock, Virginia. *Those Bad, Bad Beads.* Wilsonville, Oregon: Self-published, 1988.

Dubin, Lois Sherr. *The History of Beads.* New York: Harry N. Abrams, Inc., 1987.

Goodhue, Horace R. *Indian Bead-Weaving Patterns.* St. Paul, Minnesota: Bead-Craft, 1989.

Haertig, Evelyn. *More Beautiful Purses.* Carmel, California: Gallery Graphics Press, 1990.

Holm, Edith. *Glasperlen.* Germany: Verlag Georg D. W. Callwey, 1984.

Moss, Kathlyn, and Alice Scherer. *The New Beadwork.* New York: Harry N. Abrams, Inc., 1992.

Sarawak Museum. *Beads.* Sarawak Museum Occasional Paper No. 2. Malaysia, 1984.

Stessin, Nicolette. *Beaded Amulet Purses.* Seattle, Washington: Beadworld Publishing, 1994.

Taylor, Carol. *Creative Bead Jewelry.* New York: Sterling Publishing Co., Inc., 1995.

Thompson, Angela. *Embroidery with Beads.* London: B. T. BatsfordLtd., 1987.

van der Sleen, W. G. N. *A Handbook on Beads.* York, Pennsylvania: George Shumway.

Weber, Betty J. and Ann Duncan. *Simply Beads.* U.S.: 1971.

White, Mary. *How to Do Beadwork.* New York: Dover Publications,Inc., 1972.

Index

adding a thread, 10
African helix, 105

bead dish, 9
brick stitch, 64
bugle beads, 8

Chevron chain, 110
Comanche stitch, 64
combining stitches, 118
counting peyote rows, 13

dummy rows, 18

ending a thread, 10

findings for jewelry, 10
flush cutters, 9
fringe, making, 11; attaching to peyote, 31; attaching to brick stitch, 75

glue, 10

Japanese cylinder beads, 8

needles, beading, 9
netting, 106
Neuwirth, Waltraud, 8

peyote graph, reading, 32
peyote stitch, 12
pliers, chain-nose, 9; round-nose, 9

right-angle weave, 94
ruffles, peyote, 29

seed beads, 8
spikes, peyote, 30
square stitch, 82

tension, 15, 19
thread, beading, 9

A Note About Suppliers

Usually, the supplies you need for making the projects in Lark books can be found at your local craft supply store, discount mart, home improvement center, or retail shop relevant to the topic of the book. Occasionally, however, you may need to buy materials or tools from specialty suppliers. In order to provide you with the most up-to-date information, we have created a listing of suppliers on our Website, which we update on a regular basis. Visit us at www.larkbooks.com, click on "Craft Supply Sources," and then click on the relevant topic. You will find numerous companies listed with their web address and/or mailing address and phone number.